The Feel Better Book for Cats & Dogs

Nursing Care for All Life Stages

Randi E Golub CVT

ISBN: 1484029631
ISBN-13: 9781484029633
Library of Congress Control Number: 2013906714
CreateSpace Independent Publishing Platform
North Charleston, South Carolina

PRAISE FOR RANDI E. GOLUB'S
Sugarbabies – A Holistic Guide to Caring for Your Diabetic Pet

"As a specialist in internal medicine, I work with a number of clients who are caring for diabetic dogs and cats. It is an understatement to say that I am thrilled with Randi Golub's release of Sugarbabies. Not only is the information provided thorough and comprehensive, it is presented in a wonderfully user-friendly manner. I will be recommending Sugarbabies to all of my clients working with diabetic pets- it will make their lives easier and my job easier. Thank you so much Randi for creating this fabulous guide. Well done!"

— Dr. Nancy Kay - Author of Speaking for Spot
(Petaluma, CA, United States)

"As a veterinarian, I strongly recommend this book. Randi did a superb job of making it easy to understand for those without extensive medical knowledge, but also incredibly thorough for those who want just a little more assistance than what your veterinarian has already provided. Full of suggestions, tricks, and helpful hints, it will help answer all the questions that come up, and also improve your communication with your vet when problems do arise. It is the most user-friendly book on diabetes care that I have found. It takes away the fear and confusion surrounding this complicated disease, and will certainly improve quality of life for both pet AND owner!"

— Dr. Gail Schroder - Director of Shelter Medicine
Greenhill Humane Society (Eugene, OR, United States)

"I am a pet sitter and care for several diabetic pets. I now have more confidence that I am giving them the very best care and that I will be able to quickly spot any problems and handle emergency situations. There is so much good information included in this book and I am SO glad I found it! Thank you, Randi"

— Pat K. (Des Moines, IL, United States

"If I had only had access to a book like Sugarbabies twenty years ago, when my 8 year old cat Iris was diagnosed with diabetes, it would have made things so much easier. As it was I had to pretty much figure it out for myself. But if I'd had the knowledge that Sugarbabies gives you back then, who knows, she might have lived to be thirty! Thank you Randi Golub for writing this book for all the diabetic pet owners who only want to give them the best life possible."

— *Molly S. (Springfield, OR, United States)*

"This book is written by a Certified Vet Tech and while it deals with a very complicated disease, the author translates all the intricacies into language that is easily understood by the average pet owner. It is a very thorough look at living with a diabetic pet and all that entails. I wish this book was available in every veterinary office to aid pet parents looking at a life with a diabetic pet - they would quickly realize that it is a very manageable disease."

— *Nydia W. (Bellevue, WA, United States)*

"If you have a diabetic pet this is the book you must read. Diabetes can be a confusing subject, but Randi breaks apart the medical terminology and simplifies and explains even the most complicated processes. In her chapter on diabetic ketoacidosis she explains how to be prepared for an emergency and how to recognize key signs. The book is very detailed yet easy to read. I highly recommend this book to anyone who has to care for a diabetic pet."

— *Dr. D. Weaver (San Antonio, TX, United States)*

"When my dog was diagnosed with diabetes I was so worried! Then I found out there wasn't a lot of printed information for me to take home and read. I'm one of those people who prefer to read a book over sitting in front of a computer. I was delighted to find and share this book with my veterinarian. Sometimes I have a question at night or on weekends when their office is closed and this book has been an excellent resource for me. I enjoy Randi's writing – she has a warm and comforting style."

— *Ginger Garber (Lake Worth, FL, United States)*

⊹⊱⊰⊹

The Feel Better Book for Cats & Dogs: Nursing Care for All Life Stages

⚜

Disclaimer

The intent of this book is to help pet guardians care for and support their pets in a thoughtful and knowledgeable manner. This book is not to be used in an attempt to diagnose pets. The appropriate care and successful management of pets with health issues depends on good communication between pet guardian and veterinarian. If a pet in your care shows any signs of illness or injury, promptly seek medical advice from your veterinarian.

The author and publisher shall not be liable or responsible for any loss or damage as a result of the information contained in this book.

Introduction

I was one of those kids who always wanted to fix broken and sick animals, starting with lightning bugs, spiders, and worms in my backyard in Philadelphia. After my first job at the Philadelphia Zoo when I was fifteen, I graduated to caring for birds and orphaned baby raccoons. You never knew what you might find in my bedroom. My parents and siblings, thankfully, were supportive and got used to the odd sounds that were heard at all hours.

I am blessed to have had a long and varied career taking care of animals, and this is the book I have wanted to write for years. My love is nursing care for animals and teaching people how to best take care of their beloved companions. I am a certified veterinary technician, but I am also a Cat Mom, and I understand the stresses that arise when taking care of a sick or injured pet. I've been there. My sincere hope is to offer knowledge and suggestions that will encourage healing and good health.

The special animals in my life have taught me so much: Sesame, Violet, Choppy, Kringle, Scotty, Nubbin, Niblet, Tiki, Jimmy Jet, Chuck, Sheba, Santana, Peggy (Olive), and across-the-ocean cousins, Ginger and Niki Daube, among many others. Some of you are not with me in body anymore but live on in my heart.

I have always had a soft spot for the rescued and special needs animals in this world. And I would like to say an especially heart-felt thank you to each and every person who adopts, fosters, or sponsors one.

I dedicate this book to my late father, Samuel J. Golub, who instilled in all of his children kindness to all creatures and a love of cats. I know he would be proud.

I also dedicate this book to the late Lynne M. Maletz, VMD, and the late Abbie Moos, VMD. Both of these fine veterinarians were mentors of mine, and to this day, things they taught me still serve me well. Sadly, both left us far too soon.

Eugene, Oregon

September 2013

Acknowledgments

I would like to thank the following veterinarians for generously sharing their expertise and time by reading and clarifying the medical information contained in this book.

Liz Gray, MS, DVM

Mark McConnell, BVMS, MRCVS

Colleen Robertson, DVM

Melanie Blystone, DVM

Trish Ashley, DVM

Devon Trottier, VMD

Amy Valentine, DVM

Bert Boyden, DVM

Marla McGeorge, DVM

Devin Newman, DVM

Gail Schroder, DVM

Bob Lester, DVM

Bonnie Burns-Oberlander, DVM

Dominick A. Pulice, VMD

I would also like to thank the following friends who read, commented on, and gave great feedback on the content of this book. Your input was invaluable!

Stephen Parkinson, Julie Tanit, Christi Ridge-White, CVT, Kelly Krueger, CVT, Ann Douglass, Nydia White, Becky McDaniel, CVT, and Karen Thomas

A huge thank-you goes out to my CatNurse On Call/CatNurse Cottage clients and their wonderful pets, who have taught me volumes about nursing care, behavior, and gratitude.

I am very thankful to my photographer and friend Ken Standhardt and to his wonderful cat Bumble Standhardt -Turner and dogs Sweetpea and Cosmo Standhardt -Turner for the photographs in this book. My own Chuck along with Monte Gredigan and late Laddy Gredigan also grace these pages, so thank you.

Mary and Herb Montgomery, authors of Your Aging Pet: Making the Senior Years Healthy and Rewarding, A Final Act of Caring: Ending the Life of an Animal Friend and Good Bye My Friend: Grieving the Loss of a Pet, were kind enough to let me use their material that was previously published in *Sugarbabies*. I thank them for their generosity in let me share their writing.

And last, but certainly not least, I would like to thank my family, especially Selma Golub, Jill Golub Daube, and Lois Golub Canter, for sustaining me with encouragement and a never-ending wacky sense of humor. I love you.

CHAPTER 1
Getting Organized

What you will learn in this chapter:

- How to use a chart to stay organized

- How to organize your supplies

- What supplies are helpful to have on hand

- What an Elizabethan collar, or e-collar, is and how to make one

- Some important information about medications and treatments

Nursing care for your pet may be as simple as a once-a-day medication and simple monitoring or it may involve more intensive care such as extensively medicating, feeding, administering treatments, and writing down observations to report to your veterinarian. With our busy schedules, it can be difficult to stay organized and not feel stressed when caring for a beloved pet. Putting tools into place will help you feel more organized and alleviate the stress of having to remember what you need to do and when.

Being organized begins with having a good relationship with your veterinarian. Communication is crucial when caring for an animal with complicated or chronic health issues. It is vital that you are clear on what your home care will consist of. Often, a lot of information is discussed when a pet is discharged from the veterinary clinic. Sometimes, due to worry, it is hard to take it all in and remember what to do once you are home. Ask for a written copy of instructions, or take your own notes at this time. You'll be glad you did once you get home!

Using Charts

Making a chart can help keep you very organized and is a great way to keep others caring for your pet organized as well. No computer is needed; just use a notebook, and make columns. If several medications need to be given, a chart will help keep you organized. It will also be helpful in determining in what order to give medications. Using a chart will not only keep you on task but will also be a useful record of your pet's course of treatment. It will be handy to refer to when discussing your pet with your veterinarian on the phone or in an office visit.

Some items to include on your chart might be: date/time, names and dosages of medications, amount of subcutaneous fluids given, your pet's appetite, pain level, activity level (you can use a scale of one to ten), production of urine and feces, and what and how much have they eaten. Also leave room for comments and questions to ask your veterinarian.

Organizing Supplies

Organizing your supplies in one convenient spot will save you time. Depending on your needs, a basket, plastic shoe box, or even a small tackle box will come in very handy. A work area convenient to where you treat your pet will be helpful for storing supplies, preparing medications, and making your notes.

Your supplies may include:

- Your pet's medications, not including those that require refrigeration

- A pill cutter or pill crusher, or both

- Pet cleaning wipes for simple cleanup

- Bandaging material—cotton and gauze on a roll, self-adhesive wrap, medical tape

- Antibacterial soap such as Betadine or chlorhexidine, as recommended by your veterinarian

- 1-cc, 3-cc, or larger-sized syringes (without needles) for giving oral medications, assisted feeding, etc.

- Cotton balls or gauze squares, including nonstick gauze squares

- Disposable plastic gloves

- Thermometer and lubricant—digital thermometers are safer and faster. They often come with a flexible tip that is more comfortable for small animals.

- Stethoscope (can be purchased inexpensively online or at nursing and medical supply stores)

- Clock or watch with a second hand

- Under pads or puppy training pads—these are available as disposable or reusable

- Small hand towels for cleanup

- Comb or brush or toothbrush for cleaning the face. Flea combs also work great for this.

- Sterile bag of fluids, IV lines, needles, and a sharps container for needles, if your pet is getting subcutaneous (SC) fluids

- A chart or notebook with a pen or pencil

- Bach's Rescue Remedy® or FES Quintessentials Flower Essences Five Flower Formula® (See Chapter 2 for more information.)

- Feliway® and Comfort Zone® for dogs are products that are designed to help calm. Feliway contains a synthetic pheromone (a chemical substance produced in an animal's body) that is similar to the natural pheromones produced by cats. Cats spread this pheromone when sending friendly messages to each other. Veterinary offices and pet supply stores usually carry these products in spray and diffuser forms. Some behaviorists recommend using the spray about twenty to thirty minutes before exposing the dog or cat to Comfort Zone or Feliway, thus allowing the alcohol smell to dissipate.

- Lavender spray to use as aromatherapy (See Chapter 2)

- Scales—a postage or baby scale that weighs in ounces is important for weighing puppies and kittens

- Small, battery-operated or electric clippers for trimming fur mats, etc.

- Arsenal of special treats and food for picky eaters

- SnuggleSafe ® heating disc

(Also see Chapter 16 First Aid supplies)

Elizabethan Collar, or E-collar

You may also want to have on hand an e-collar in the appropriate size to fit your pet. An e-collar is a collar made of rigid plastic or other stiff material. It prevents an animal from biting or licking itself. Often, pets recovering from surgery need to wear an e-collar to prevent them from licking at incisions and biting at sutures (stitches) or bandages. An e-collar is also very useful when treating skin problems such as irritations and hot spots that pets tend to lick too much.

There are many styles and sizes of e-collars, including a soft, thick e-collar. E-collars are available from veterinary offices and pet supply stores. You can also make your own at home in an emergency situation, such as on weekends and in the middle of the night, when an animal needs to be restrained from biting or licking.

To make your own e-collar, take a piece of cardboard or rigid plastic, and cut it in a conical shape. Tape the short edges to each other. Punch holes along the part that will go closest to your pet's neck. Weave a shoelace or other strip of material through the holes, and tie it around your pet's neck so the collar does not fall off and your pet cannot remove it. Also make sure your pet's nose can stick out and that there are no sharp edges that can irritate or cut the skin. It is important that you are able to slide your fingers between the collar and the pet's neck, indicating that the collar is not secured too tightly.

A simple e-collar for small animals can be made in a pinch by cutting a hole in a cardboard plate and lining the hole with duct tape so the rough edge does not cut the pet's skin. This can then be slipped over the pet's head until a sturdier e-collar can be obtained. A large e-collar can be made by cutting a hole in the bottom of a plastic bucket and slipping it over the pet's head. Line the cut edges with duct tape to prevent irritation from the sharp edge.

E-collars are also affectionately called "party hats" or not so affectionately called "the cone of shame" ☺

Medications

Make sure that every medication is clearly labeled with directions and that you and anyone caring for your pet understands them. A bottle labeled only "Use as directed" is not only illegal but also will not be helpful to anyone but you (as long as you remember exactly what was meant.) Make sure you know when and when not to give your pet's medications. Some medications need to be given in a specific order so that their effectiveness is not diminished. For example, giving a medication that coats the lining of the stomach may hamper the absorption of another medication given at the same time. Also, some eye medications will need to be given in a certain order to be effective. For more information on medicating your pet, please see Chapter 9.

Treatments

It is also important to be clear on your pet's treatment instructions. You may need to clean a wound, apply a compress, monitor an incision, give fluids, do assisted feeding, offer short periods of exercise, or even express a bladder. More information can be found on these procedures throughout this book. Recording these treatments on your chart will help to keep you organized so you will be able to better judge the time needed for doing them without rushing. Pets can easily pick up on our feelings, and they will be more calm and accepting of what you need to do if it is done with as little stress as possible.

Now you have your supplies organized, your chart or notebook, and a comfortable work space. With an organized game plan, you can now concentrate on providing the very best care for your pet.

In Chapter 4 you will learn about your role as caretaker. The role of the caretaker can be overwhelming and tiring and, yet, one of the most important jobs you will ever have.

The bond we have with beloved pets is strengthened by the unconditional love we receive from them. They are often our best friends, and we think nothing of expending huge amounts of emotional and physical energy supporting them in a health crisis.

Step back and take a deep breath—you are on your way to providing the care and TLC your pet needs. You will be an excellent nurse!

cW

CHAPTER 2

Providing a Lovely and Loving Environment for Your Pet

What you will learn in this chapter:

ᐛ **What a healthy environment for a healing or recovering pet is**

ᐛ **Why sleep is important and how to encourage it**

ᐛ **How to create a comfortable environment for your pet**

Can you remember a time when you had the flu or an illness that kept you bedridden for an extended amount of time? After awhile, the air in the room felt stale, the sheets were cruddy, there was stuff jumbled up on the night table, and all around you there was the feeling of disease. Getting out of that environment was an incentive to get better! Cats and dogs are very sensitive creatures and can also suffer from an environment that promotes illness, not wellness. Whether it is for a short or long period of time, preparing a comfortable and pleasant place for your pet is an act of love you will both appreciate.

A Healthy, Restful Environment

Your pet will appreciate a place that:

ᐛ Is out of the main traffic area in the house but not well out of sight. You need to monitor your pet, and they will benefit from hearing familiar voices and noises that keep them feeling like a part of the family. If your pet is bedridden or immobile, you may choose to have several quiet areas where they can rest. A change of scenery throughout the day will provide mental stimulation. Monitor them for signs of stress wherever you choose to keep them. Signs of stress may include restlessness, vocalizing, panting, pacing, and yawning or licking their lips (in dogs), cowering, and trying to hide under bedding. Moving them to a quieter place will be more restful for them. If crate rest is required, your pet can have its own little den and still feel like a part of the family. (See Chapter 3 for more information on crate rest.)

- ❧ Keeps them being close to the family and other pets and is also safe from other household pets who may not act kindly now that they smell and act different. While some animals are protective and caring of a disabled pet, they can also be confused by the changes in the animal's smells and actions. They may react strongly, even if they were formerly buddies. It is not unusual for them to show aggression by stalking, growling, or hissing at an animal that is their friend. Use baby gates, crates, or other boundaries to keep your recovering pet safe from other pets in the house.

- ❧ Is an appropriate temperature. The ideal temperature for house pets is around seventy to eighty degrees Fahrenheit (twenty one to twenty six degrees Celsius) and around 50 percent humidity. Good ventilation is important, but a chilly, drafty place is not healthy for your pet. Unless the air outside is frigid and your pet's temperature is already low, a little fresh air for a short period of time will refresh your pet and its environment. Bear in mind, young and old animals are more susceptible to temperature extremes. They also may be compromised in regulating their body temperature and may get chilly quicker. In the summer, ventilation is especially important.

Cats and dogs do not sweat the way we do, and it is very important that you make sure they are not overheated. Use air conditioning on a low setting or use a fan to generate moving air around your pet if the room temperature is high. Heavy-coated animals and animals such as Persian cats, Pugs, Pekingese, and other *braceocephalic* breeds are more susceptible to heat. Brachycephalic literally means "shortened head." These animals have a unique anatomy that prevents them from taking in air as well as other animals. They need to be monitored very closely for signs of heat stress. (See Chapter 16 for heat-related emergencies).

Dogs will often seek cool surfaces such as tile or concrete flooring when ill, while cats often seek heat. It is important to pay attention to the individual animal's instinctive needs as opposed to what we think is best for them.

- Is convenient if you have to carry your dog outside to relieve itself or to get fresh air.

- Is an area without a TV or computer. Both emit blue light that can suppress the production of melatonin. Melatonin is a hormone secreted in the brain that helps regulate an animal's sleep-wake cycles.

- Has some of its favorite things nearby. Although your pet may not feel like playing, a favorite mouse or ball, or even your sweater or T-shirt, may be of comfort.

Time for Rest

As the saying goes, it is important to let a sleeping dog (and cat) lie. Rest and uninterrupted sleep are essential for any animal's well-being, especially those recovering from illness or injury. If your pet has just come from the hospital, it may not have slept well and will really appreciate the comfort of sleeping in its own home. Although the continual monitoring in an emergency hospital is essential in many cases, it may not have been especially restful for your pet.

Limit the interaction the family has with your pet when your pet comes home. Although it will be exciting to have your pet back, what your pet needs now is peace and quiet.

If your pet is restless, pacing, or vocalizing, pain may be an issue. Discuss this with your veterinarian to see if pain medication needs to be added or if perhaps the dose needs to be adjusted. An animal that is in pain and not able to settle down will not be able to get the rest it needs to recover and heal. (See Chapter 20 for information on signs of pain.)

Lighting

Natural light is the best choice for lighting in your pet's area whenever possible. Allowing for natural day and night cycles is also important. Do not leave the lights on all night; your pet needs darkness to sleep well. Just like with us, morning or early afternoon light can have an energizing effect on our pets. When considering artificial sources, choose lighting that is practical and soothing. Full-spectrum lighting is the best as it is the most natural. These are the types of lights that are used for growing plants. Full-spectrum lights have been thought to stimulate the body's production of melatonin. Melatonin is a hormone produced in the body that helps control sleep and wake cycles. Melatonin has been used by some veterinarians to treat behavior problems due to pain, anxiety, and fear. It may also help promote good sleep in older animals. **Please check with your veterinarian, and never give your pet melatonin that is meant for human use.**

Monitoring a wound, bandage, or a patient's gum color requires good lighting. A task lamp may be perfect for this and used as needed. Soft lighting in tones of red or amber promotes restfulness. Provide night-lights throughout the area to make navigating at night easier for all pets, not only those with diminishing eyesight. An excellent choice for lighting in your pet's recovery area is a salt lamp. Not only does a salt lamp provide tranquil and soothing lighting, but it may also help clean the air through ionization and can help neutralize electromagnetic wavelengths that come from electronic devices. Salt lamps come in a variety of colors and have been suggested to promote healing of the mind and body.

Music

Some pets show a distinct reaction to music. Gentle, rhythmic music such as light jazz, classical, or harp music played softly may be relaxing to your pet. Recent studies have shown harp music to be a "valuable enrichment therapy that affects pets and people." Some of the potential benefits of harp music may include lower heart rate, pulse, blood pressure, and respiration, as well as decreased anxiety and stress. Quicker surgical recovery times, improved digestion, and improved immune function are also potential benefits. Everyone wins when listening to this music—as we feel calmer, our pets feel calmer, and vice versa. Harp music can even make treatment and medicating times go much easier for all involved.

Avoid subjecting your pet to sounds they may find startling and unsettling such as construction noise, a loud boom box or TV, slamming doors, and loud voices.

Aromatherapy

Although aromatherapy uses natural substances such as essential oils, much care must be taken when using them with your pets. Animals, especially cats, can be very sensitive to essential oils. It is best to consult with a person trained in knowing which essential oils can be safely used around your pets.

One simple aromatherapy recipe involves lavender. Lavender has been proven to reduce stress and has many applications when working with animals. The author's favorite use is obtained by adding several drops of lavender essential oil to a spray bottle of spring water. The lightly scented water can be used to mist the bedding of a pet or misted on a hand towel and placed near bedding. Just like with harp music, it benefits both pet and caretaker. When working with soft lighting, harp music, and lavender, a relaxing state is not far away.

Flower Essences

There are many single-flower essences that can help treat and support animals. Bach's Rescue Remedy® and FES Quintessentials Flower Essences Five Flower Formula® are formulas that include the same blend of five flower essences specially chosen to help animals who are recovering from illness or injury or during stressful times. These liquid formulas can naturally and gently help reduce stress in your pet (and you as well). They can safely be used before giving injections, traveling, visiting the vet, or in the extreme case your pet is suffering from seizures or trauma. (They are not meant to replace appropriate medical care but can help while on the way to the veterinarian.) These products can be mixed in canned food, added to the water bowl, given by mouth (although some animals may dislike the taste), or rubbed onto the ears. Only a few drops are needed, whichever way you choose to administer it. It can also be added to a spray bottle of spring water (add about a dropperful) and sprayed in the room, carrier, car, or area where you will be doing injections or treatments.

By providing a healing place for recovery or a comforting place for hospice care, your pet will benefit from the thoughtfulness you have put into providing for its needs. And while they can't say thank you, a gentle purr or lick of the hand speaks volumes.

✤

CHAPTER 3
Keeping Your Pet Comfortable

What you will learn in this chapter:

🐾 What kind of bedding works well for a recovering pet

🐾 What decubital (pressure) sores are and how to prevent them

🐾 How to keep a pet warm and dry

🐾 What crate rest is and how to make it successful

Every creature appreciates a comfortable place to rest. Animals that are recovering from illness or injury or those in a hospice situation will spend a lot of time lying down and resting. Before your pet comes home from the hospital, make sure you have bedding all set up for it. Your pet will appreciate the extra care you have put into making it as comfortable as possible upon its return.

Bedding

The ideal bedding is:

🐾 Comfortable and appropriate for your pet's needs and wants. A pet recovering with a cast on its leg will need to stretch out comfortably, while another pet may want to curl up in an enclosed or donut-shaped bed.

🐾 Washable! All sorts of things may get on your pet's bedding, and it will require machine washing. Your pet will appreciate a clean bed, and it will be more hygienic. Avoid beds that say "spot-clean only." Make sure you have a spare for when one bed is in the wash.

๛ Inexpensive. There are many inexpensive ways to make an ideal bed for your pet.

Bedding for Incontinent or Immobile Pets to Avoid Decubital Sores

Keeping an immobile or incontinent pet dry and clean is a must. Urine and feces that remain on the skin and fur can cause irritation and are breeding grounds for germs and infections.

Puppy training pads and underpads for human use are relatively inexpensive, disposable, and practical for use in many cases. These can be bought in bulk at pet supply and human medical supply stores. Unfortunately, they also generate a large amount of trash. Machine washable and reusable incontinence pads are an ideal solution. Most thrift stores sell perfectly fine bedding and towels that can also be used. One of the best choices for bedding is machine washable fake lambswool or thick fleece. Both are especially useful as they whisk moisture away from an animal. They are also warm and cushioning. Note: You may not always be able to see when they become wet with urine, so feeling them several times a day is highly recommended.

Bedding for immobile pets must be highly cushioned to avoid the formation of decubital (pressure) sores. These are sores that develop on pressure points such as elbows, ankles, and hips. This type of deep sore can eventually expose the bone and make a pet more likely to develop a bone infection. If you notice these sores forming, discuss them with your veterinarian, as padding or bandaging these areas may be needed.

Many thickly padded beds are commercially available, although you can easily and inexpensively make your own. Many fabric or medical supply stores sell egg crate or high-density foam. These can be cut to size, topped with an absorbent pad, and slipped into a thrift store pillow sham. Voila! A practical, inexpensive, and stylish new bed for your pet! Thrift and secondhand stores are a great source for usable and inexpensive pillow shams in a wide range of fabrics, sizes, and colors. Large or heavy pets may require commercially made beds that accommodate their weight appropriately.

A child's or twin-size blow-up air mattress makes an excellent and inexpensive bed for an immobile large pet. It is lightweight, easily cleaned, and waterproof, and it provides a soft but firm surface for your pet to lie on. To avoid punctures, make sure your pet's nails are trimmed and the bed is completely and thickly covered.

Heated Beds

Heated beds are useful for young and elderly patients as well as patients who are not able to regulate their body temperatures. Animals who tend to be chilly and arthritic will really appreciate a heated bed. It is very important to make sure an animal can easily move off of or out of a heated bed, should it feel too warm.

Although it may be tempting to use your heating pad, beds and warming inserts made specifically for pets are a much safer choice. Immobile pets, pets with very short fur, and pets with thin or exposed skin are at great risk of being burned by a heating pad that is too warm.

If your pet is constantly moving off of the nice warm bed you have provided, it may just feel too warm. Allow it to get settled where it chooses, provided it is a safe and comfortable place.

Other options for keeping your pet warm are a SnuggleSafe, warmed rice sack, or hot-water bottles. A SnuggleSafe is a microwavable disc that retains heat for up to nine hours. Take caution when using these as they can be very hot. It is important to make sure a thick layer is between the disc and your pet and that your pet can move away from it if it feels too warm. You can make your own rice sack. Fill an athletic sock with rice (flaxseed works well, too), knot it at the top, and warm it in the microwave. The advantage to using the Snuggle Safe or rice sack is that they both slowly lose heat and do not get cold, as do hot-water bottles. When using hot-water bottles, make sure they do not leak and remove them when they cool down so your pet is not resting on a chilly surface.

Under the Bedding

There are several solutions to keeping the floor under the bedding dry and clean. Hard plastic floor mats, such as those used under office chairs, a large piece of marine vinyl (sold in fabric or marine supply stores), as well as hard plastic carpet runner (sold in home improvement and flooring supply stores) will all keep your flooring around your pet dry and clean.

Thick rubber mats can be used to insulate your pet from a chilly floor. Dri-Dek is a type of perforated rubber matting that works very well for this purpose. Dri-Dek keeps pets dry and comfortable by allowing liquids to drain away from the bedding and by allowing air to circulate under the pet.

Changing Bedding

Depending on the nature of the situation, changing your pets' bedding should be done as often as needed to provide them with a clean and fresh-smelling environment. If you are concerned about moving your pet that may be recovering from surgery, ask your veterinary technician to show you how to appropriately lift it. It will take two people to move larger dogs quickly and efficiently. Never roll an animal over on its back to change soiled bedding.

Crate Rest

Occasionally, a pet will be put on crate or kennel rest while recovering from surgery. This means the animal needs to be kept confined to the kennel or crate, except for being taken out for urinating, defecating, and receiving treatments. While crate rest can be very difficult for the caretaker to follow, not complying with this may mean a setback in healing and recovery. To make a kennel or crate cozier, an infant's crib bumper is a great way to cushion the sides of the crate and to provide a softer and warmer environment. They can almost always be found in abundance in thrift stores. Providing enrichment for these confined pets, especially puppies and kittens, may be challenging, but it is important to find toys that strike the balance between stimulation and quiet play. Hiding low-calorie treats in toys made just for this purpose can help keep a restless animal entertained. Your pet should still have a pleasant and comfortable place to call its temporary home, even during times of confinement.

Crate rest is often recommended for pets that are recovering from orthopedic surgery or injuries to a bone or bones. Although it may not seem so, bones are living parts of any animal's body. Broken bones begin to repair quickly after an injury. In very simplified terms, small blood clots form immediately on the edges of a broken bone, beginning the mending process. Among other functions, they help to stabilize the bone. Tiny blood vessels grow into the place where the clots are now formed and help to nourish newly forming tissue. This new tissue is called a *soft callus*. Other cells come in to produce *collagen*, followed by formation of *fibrocartilage*. This is followed by the formation of *fibrocartilaginous callus,* which forms the bridge between the pieces of broken bone. The next step is the formation of a hard shell called *bone callus*. This callus protects and stabilizes the bone in the final stages of mending. All of these processes are leading toward the eventual complete healing of the bone. Too much movement can disrupt these processes, causing your pet's bone healing to be greatly delayed or, in some cases, to heal improperly. While it can be difficult to confine your pet during the healing process, it is very important! The proper confinement for a healing pet means following instructions for crate rest as well as not allowing your pet to be too active (or in some cases be allowed to walk) when it is outside of the crate.

Keeping a pet with a broken bone immobile (along with giving prescribed pain medication) will help to lessen its pain. Controlling pain is vitally important for many reasons. Not only is it the humane thing to do, but also recent studies have shown that pain relief promotes healing. When pain is uncontrolled, healing time is longer, the immune system is depressed, and pets may not get the sleep that is vitally important for repairing injuries and for well-being. Treating pain also improves the general health of the pet. It may improve appetite, enable the pet to be more mobile, and reduce time in the hospital.

For more information on the signs of pain, please see Chapter 20.

After you have gotten your pet settled into its comfy bed with a kiss and words of love and encouragement, it's time for lights out and sweet dreams. Imagine your pet's delight when it wakes up after a restorative sleep and realizes—"I'm home!"

o✧o

CHAPTER 4

Taking Care of the Caretaker

What you will learn in this chapter:

ఆ How to take good care of yourself when caring for an ill or injured animal

ఆ What some of the emotions you may feel are

Taking Good Care of Yourself

How important it is to stay balanced and healthy, especially when the demands of caretaking are the greatest, cannot be overestimated. Your pet depends on you so entirely for its well-being, and you owe it to the both of you to take good care of yourself.

Some days will be easier than others. There will be days when you will need to rely not only on your own strength but also on that of supportive friends and family. Surround yourself with the good energy that comes from people who understand your feelings and what your pet means to you.

Here are some things you can do for yourself:

ఆ Take time out to eat well, not just quick meals on the run. Good nutrition will help to sustain you.

ఆ Make sure you get plenty of rest. Sleep is vital for recharging and replenishing energy.

- Exercising regularly (even when you don't feel like it) will help provide you with a sense of well-being and will help to decrease stress. Bribe yourself if you must, but get to the gym or go out for a walk. You'll feel much better afterward.

- Try to get some "me time" every day. Take a walk, browse in a bookstore, work in the garden, get a massage, or just rest on the couch with a good book. Whatever you choose to do, make sure it's all about you!

- Find inspiration wherever feels right to you—nature, art, music, or religion.

- Treat yourself to something special; you work hard, and you deserve it.

- Don't forget to laugh. Laughter is good medicine. Watch a funny movie, or listen to a favorite comedian. It's not only OK to laugh during hard times, but it's important that you do.

Accepting Your Emotions

Often, people will offer to help in any way they can. Take them up on it. With animals that are at the end of their lives or those that require a high degree of monitoring, you may find it difficult to leave their sides. Having a friend sit in for you will provide you with a chance to get some fresh air, run some errands, or just get a little time to yourself. Take this time out, especially during very stressful times, for it will help refresh your spirit.

Some people choose to share their feelings with a good friend while others may prefer to record their feelings in a journal. It is important to let off some steam from time to time and know that *all* your feelings are valid, not just the nice ones. A vigorous workout, a brisk walk, or, if you are like me, cleaning the house will offer a release for pent-up emotions.

Be flexible and realistic in understanding your pet's condition or illness. There may be disappointments and setbacks. You may at times feel like you are on an emotional roller coaster. So as hard as it may be, allow things to unfold as they will.

Animals live in the moment. They don't worry about tomorrow or worry about dying. Through them, we can learn the importance of taking each minute for what it is.

Above all, remember that the time we spend with our pets is a special gift and a chance to shower them with all the love in our hearts. Now is the time to make your time together, for as long as you may have together, the best it can be.

࿇

CHAPTER 5
Your Pet's Medical History

What you will learn in this chapter:

ஃ **How to find a veterinary team that works for you**

ஃ **What your pet's medical record includes**

ஃ **What commonly run diagnostic tests are**

You and Your Veterinary Team

Having a good relationship with your veterinary team is very important. Especially when you have a chronically or seriously ill pet, you will need to work closely and harmoniously in your pet's best interest. Not all veterinarians are the same, and some styles work better with certain people than others. Some veterinarians like to talk and explain things, while some owners just want basic treatment and no explanations. Some veterinarians are excellent doctors but short on explanations, while some people love to hear all the details!

You should treat your relationship with your veterinarian and staff as any other long-term relationship. If you only go in once every five years with a dying pet, compared to a regular relationship, there may be differences in the veterinarian's abilities to understand and to treat your pet.

How do you find a good veterinary team? Below are some ideas that may be helpful:

- Ask friends, family, and coworkers for recommendations. Ask them what they like about their veterinarian and their staff.

- For some people, e-mailing is a very important part of communicating with their veterinarian. Ask if this is an option.

- Are the hours, location, and methods of payment convenient for you?

- Are there discounts for seniors, service animals, or multi-pet households?

- Are the cats and dogs housed in different areas? Your cat will appreciate this if it needs to be hospitalized.

- Is the facility clean, well-organized, and comfortable? This does not mean it has to be fancy.

- Is the hospital AAHA certified? The American Animal Hospital Association was founded in 1933 and provides voluntary accreditation to companion animal hospitals. AAHA-certified hospitals have made a commitment to meeting the highest standards of veterinary care.

Your veterinarian and their staff will appreciate if you:

- Treat them with courtesy even when you are scared, worried, or frustrated.

- Show up on time for your appointments and surgery drop-offs.

- Have your pet appropriately restrained; use a collar/harness and leash or a pet carrier.

- Turn off your phone, especially when you are in the exam room!

- Are mentally invested in your pet's appointment.

- Act as an advocate for your pet!

- Call ahead for prescription refills.

- Call ahead in an emergency situation to see if a veterinarian is available. If one is not, you may be referred to an emergency facility. While this may be frustrating, it is for your pet's well-being.

- Understand that the Internet is a great source of information, some of which needs to be taken with a grain of salt.

Your Pet's Medical History

It is recommended that cats and dogs be examined by a veterinarian at least once a year (or as soon as possible when health issues arise). At this time, your veterinarian will take a complete medical history and ask you many questions about your pet's lifestyle and habits. Your veterinarian may also discuss behavioral issues with you. Next, he or she will do a complete physical exam, which includes looking at external parts such as the ears, eyes, teeth, skin, and general appearance of your pet. He or she will evaluate the heart, lungs, and abdomen and also feel for any swellings, lumps, or other abnormalities. The history taking and physical exam may be fairly brief or, in the case of a young or old animal, more lengthy. This is the best time to ask questions and address issues that you are noticing in your pet.

Your pet's medical history may include:

- Date of examination

- Signalment (owner and pet identification)

- Presenting complaint (reason for the exam)

- Past medical history

- History of present illness (or if this is a yearly or well-animal exam)

- Current health status

- Systems review: your veterinarian will ask questions about major body systems, such as whether there is any coughing or sneezing, vomiting, or diarrhea.

- Pet's family history (history of parents and littermates)

- Vaccination and deworming history

- Has your kitten or cat been tested for FeLV/FIV?

- Has your dog or cat been tested for heartworm disease?

- Has your pet had a recent fecal test?

- Travel history: is your pet from another part of the country, or do you travel with it?

- Diet history: What do you feed your pet?

- Environmental history: indoor only, outdoor only, indoor/outdoor?

There are times when certain symptoms or behaviors that you report may prompt your veterinarian to suggest running diagnostic tests such as blood work, urinalysis (complete analysis of the urine), or fecal (feces) tests.

When to Test

As part of establishing a good medical history on your pet, your veterinarian will ask about your pet's daily habits, including its eating and drinking. Perhaps you have told your vet that your older cat seems to be drinking more than normal or your dog seems to have forgotten its house training. Because excessive drinking and urinating are classic signs of several diseases, your vet will want to run blood work to help make the correct diagnosis of what is going on with your pet. Your long-haired cat may look the same to you but weigh three pounds less than last year. Because weight loss is another common symptom, your veterinarian will want to run blood work to help find out the cause.

Blood work and urinalysis are also recommended for all cats and dogs over eight years old (or earlier for a large-breed dog) even if a specific problem is not noted. Blood work is routinely run to establish baseline information. Baseline information is your pet's health status is when your pet is healthy. It will also be used at a later date to see how your pet is responding to treatment or to see the progression of any problems. It is basically a starting point from which to monitor your pet's health.

Commonly Requested Tests

Commonly requested blood tests are serum chemistry tests (CHEM) and complete blood counts (CBC). Serum is the liquid portion of the blood, without cells. Serum chemistry tests check the status of organ function, electrolytes, and blood glucose levels, as well as check for other conditions and diseases. Complete blood counts check the numbers, sizes, and types of red and white blood cells that give information on hydration status, anemia, infection, and the immune system's efficiency. Whole blood also includes platelets. Numbers of platelets are counted to assess the blood's ability to clot.

Other blood tests are done to check thyroid function, especially in older animals. In their later years, cats are prone to hyperthyroidism, while dogs are prone to hypothyroidism. Simply put, hyperthyroidism is when the thyroid is over active while hypothyroidism is when the thyroid is underactive. To assure as accurate a test as possible, follow your veterinarian's request to make your pet fast before testing, if at all possible.

Cats should be tested for feline leukemia virus (FeLV) and feline immunodeficiency virus (FIV). Dogs and cats in high-risk areas should be tested for heartworm disease.

Urine Testing

As part of establishing your pet's current health condition, your veterinarian may also request that a urinalysis be run. A complete urinalysis includes two parts. The first is using a urine reagent strip that determines the presence of glucose, protein, red and white blood cells, bilirubin, and ketones. (The presence of ketones helps to identify a condition called *diabetic ketoacidosis* or DKA.) Second, the pH levels and specific gravity (concentration) of the urine are tested. Microscopic examination of the urine sample is used to look for urinary crystals, cells, bacteria, casts, and other indicators of a problem. (However, current thinking is that a certain number of crystals may be a normal finding.)

Additional information can be found when a urine culture and sensitivity is run. A urine culture is a method used to grow and identify bacteria that may be causing a urinary tract infection. The sensitivity test enables veterinarians to prescribe the correct antibiotic to treat the infection.

There are several methods for collecting urine. If the test is only for glucose and ketones, a sterile sample is not needed.

Cystocentesis—This method is used when a sterile urine sample is needed and is done in the hospital. Both cats and dogs usually tolerate this procedure well from a lying down position, although some dogs may be more comfortable standing up. The veterinarian or technician will first palpate to feel the urinary bladder. The bladder feels like a small water balloon when full. They will then insert a sterile needle into the bladder through the abdominal wall and withdraw urine. If you know that your pet is going to have this procedure done, putting extra water in its food or offering broth can help it arrive at the hospital with a full bladder. When taking your cat into the hospital for this procedure, do not put a towel or cloth in the carrier. Your cat may be less inclined to urinate in the carrier if there is nothing soft in it. One veterinarian has observed that cats seem to urinate after eating. She recommends that her patients not feed their cats if bringing them into the hospital for an early morning urine sample. With a diabetic cat, this could be a concern, so check with your vet before withholding your pet's food.

Free catch—This method is used when a urine sample need not be sterile or when other methods of obtaining urine are unsuccessful. The urine is caught in a cup or flat container while the animal is urinating or is obtained from a clean litter box. This method is used at home or in the hospital. See Chapter 15 for detailed instructions on getting a urine sample from a cat or dog.

Fecal Testing

Fecal tests also help to establish baseline information. For good health, your pet needs to be free from internal parasites as well as bacterial overgrowth. Information obtained from a fecal sample can help give your veterinarian a lot of information about your pet's health and can help determine the cause of illness.

See Chapter 15 on how to collect a fecal sample.

Because disease is not always apparent due to the fact that animals can be very good at masking symptoms and it can be hard to monitor their symptoms, these tests are important parts of establishing your pet's complete health profile.

oᴥo

CHAPTER 6

Nutrition and Feeding Your Pet

What you will learn in this chapter:

ᴥ What probiotics are and why they can be beneficial

ᴥ What food is best for your pet

ᴥ What carbohydrates are and whether your pet needs them

ᴥ The benefits of canned or fresh food versus dry food

ᴥ What a raw food diet is

ᴥ What a homemade diet should be

ᴥ How to feed your pet

ᴥ How to transition pets to a new food

ᴥ How to encourage your pet to eat

ᴥ How to feed an emaciated animal

ᴥ How to make your own baby food

Nutrition is a very important part of maintaining good health for any pet. The best diet will provide good overall nutrition and the appropriate amount of calories while supporting weight loss or weight gain if necessary. It is critical that animals get proper nutrition in order to recover from disease, illness, or injury, to fight infection, and to heal properly.

Pet foods should include high-quality, highly digestible sources of protein such as chicken, turkey, beef, lamb, or fish. Protein is essential for functions such as muscle growth, maintenance of tissues, reproduction, and energy. Although it is a source of much discussion, whole grains may also be added to supply complex carbohydrates that in turn supply energy. Many pet foods also include fruits and vegetables that add antioxidants, enzymes, vitamins, minerals, and fiber, all of which promote good health.

Food should be as fresh as possible. Many animals will turn their noses down at food that is even slightly "off." Food should be room temperature or, better yet, warm. Warm food is more natural for a pet to eat and will smell more tempting. Experiment with different textures to see what your pet's preference is. Some animals, cats especially, do not like chunky food; they like it smooth.

Probiotics

There are two types of bacteria that live in our intestinal systems and that of our pets, beneficial and harmful bacteria. The beneficial bacteria ensure good health and help to maintaining the correct balance of good and bad bacteria in the gut. A course of antibiotics, illness, change of food, and stress can throw off the balance. Probiotics are beneficial bacteria that can help restore the balance. Below is a list of just a few of the important functions of probiotics:

- Regulate and stimulate parts of the immune system

- Inhibit the growth of some yeast

- Remove toxins ingested through foods

- Remove toxins as waste products of digestion

- Reduce food intolerance

- Reduce inflammation

- Promote good digestion of food

- Produce natural antibiotics, which can protect against harmful bacteria

Many quality pet foods contain probiotics in their formulas. Probiotics can also be added to pet foods in the form of flavored sprinkles that pets enjoy. A tablespoon of fresh, high-quality yogurt given daily can also be beneficial to your pet. *Lactobacillus acidophilus*, *Bifidobacterium bifidum*, and *Lactobacillus bulgaricus* are some of the good bacteria that you will see included.

Best Foods for Your Pet

How do you know what diet is best for your pet? There are many healthy foods on the market today that will provide excellent nutrition to the entire animal while supporting specific conditions, such as diabetes, cancer, or kidney disease. When choosing a diet for your pet, consider your own philosophy on nutrition along with what will benefit your pet. If *you* would not eat by-products and unhealthy ingredients, would you want to feed them to your pet, especially considering there are more healthy alternatives? If you believe in consuming organic, fresh foods, you can choose a pet food containing only these types of ingredients. These types of food can be found at holistic veterinary offices and at pet supply stores specializing in these types of products.

In general, good choices for any pet's diet are foods free of by-products and low-quality sources of fat and protein (all of which may come from "4D animals"—dead, diseased, disabled, or dying), artificial flavors and colors, as well as fillers such as corn and wheat products. Learn how to read a pet food label (see the resource section for more information) so you will have a better idea of exactly what your pet is ingesting. A good quality source of protein should be the first ingredient and should say, for example, "chicken" or "chicken meal." Any grains present should be at least third or fourth on the list.

Many people feel the best diet for any pet is one that is well-balanced with high-quality ingredients and that it will reliably eat. There is no sense in feeding a food your pet will not enjoy and will not eat consistently, even if it is a "prescription" food. There are so many choices on the market today; by doing your homework and asking questions, you can find the right diet for your pet.

Do Pets Need Carbohydrates?

There is much debate over whether cats and dogs need carbohydrates. Many veterinarians and nutritionists alike believe that dogs and cats can live healthfully without carbohydrates if the diet supplies enough energy in the form of glucose. Glucose can be obtained from other sources, such as fat or protein. Because carbohydrates are easier to use, they are converted to energy (glucose) first, before protein and fats. In this way, the amount of carbohydrates present regulates how much protein and fat will be broken down and used for energy. When there is an overabundance of carbohydrates, fat is stored instead of used. When there are not enough carbohydrates, fat will be converted and used. When there are no carbohydrates present, then fat *and* protein are used for energy.

Grain is a source of carbohydrates. Proponents for including grain in a pet's diet state that in the wild, cats and dogs eat animals such as birds and small rodents. These animals eat various seeds and grains. When a cat or dog ingests these animals, they are also ingesting the partially digested grain contents from the stomachs of their prey. But this grain is vastly different from the over processed, fractionated grains that make up the majority of some pet foods. In general, many dry foods have high levels of grain. When feeding a pet food containing grains, it is recommended that grains do not exceed 10 percent of the total ingredients.

Cats and dogs are not as efficient in digesting carbohydrates as we are. They do not have enzymes in their mouths that begin to break down carbohydrates, the way we do. They also have digestive tracts that are much shorter than ours.

Cats and other members of the superfamily *Feloidea* are obligate carnivores. This means they have strict requirements for certain nutrients that can only be found in animal tissues, such as taurine and arginine, both amino acids. Cats *must* eat meat and should never be offered a vegetarian diet. They should also never be fed dog food, as nutritional deficiencies will occur.

Cats are designed to use protein as their main source of energy, not carbohydrates, and may have trouble digesting carbohydrates. Reducing or eliminating carbs in a diabetic cat's diet usually results in improved glucose metabolism. For this reason, many cats can resolve their diabetes through diet alone.

Dogs are taxonomically classified as carnivores, although their ability to thrive on meat, grains, and vegetables makes them, in a dietary sense, omnivores. However, grains are not a necessary or an evolutionary component of their diet.

A low-carbohydrate diet will also support the health of the pancreas. The pancreas has to work overtime producing insulin to counteract the effects of too much sugar (which is produced by carbohydrates) and producing enzymes to counteract the effects of too much fat. A low-carbohydrate and low-fat diet places the least amount of stress on the pancreas.

Dry Foods (Kibble)

While convenient and economical for many people, diets consisting exclusively of dry foods are increasingly suspected for causing many common pet diseases such as diabetes, obesity, inflammatory bowel disease, urinary blockage, and kidney disease. Levels of carbohydrates are often very high in dry pet food. This, coupled with subpar ingredients, makes dry food no bargain when you are trying to offer your pet an appropriate food that will support good health throughout its life.

Cats especially should not be fed a diet of exclusively dry food. Cats are animals that originally descended from the desert. Their kidneys became very efficient in order to conserve water. The mainstay of their diet was fresh prey, which consisted of about 70 percent moisture. The dry food that they eat now is usually in the range of 7 to 10 percent moisture. Many veterinarians feel that, as a result, most cats live their lives in a state of constant dehydration, which puts a strain on the kidneys and can account for kidney failure later in life.

Canned and Fresh Foods

As a pet ages, feeding fresh and canned foods is even more important as a way of getting more water into its system. Fresh and canned foods should be the majority of every older cat's and dog's diet. We have created a nation of dry-pet-food junkies, and it is well worth persevering to find other types of foods that your pet will enjoy. Feeding fresh and canned foods will especially help diabetic pets and will help all pets avoid dehydration.

You can get more moisture into your pet's diet by adding some of the following to their regular diet:

- Canned food

- Cooked chicken or turkey breast

- Low-fat plain yogurt

- Cottage cheese

- Organ meats such as heart, liver, or kidneys

- Gizzards

- Steamed vegetables such as squash or broccoli. Grinding helps break down cellulose and makes raw vegetables more digestible for pets.

In Chapter 8, you will find more suggestions for increasing water consumption.

Raw Food Diets

A subject of controversy is the feeding of a raw food diet to cats and dogs. Some veterinarians and nutritionists believe that is vitally important for animals to ingest raw meat, while some veterinarians feel that it is an unsafe and nutritionally lacking diet. To supporters of this type of diet, there is no doubt that this is a more healthy and natural way to feed pets, although there are some concerns and considerations. There are precautions that you need to take as well as questions to ask yourself when considering if this is a diet you can safely provide to your pet.

Raw food diets should not be fed:

- To animals with compromised immune systems—very young, elderly, or ill animals

- If sanitation is an issue. No one should be allowed to handle the food without thoroughly washing hands afterward. Food must be stored and served correctly.

- By immune-compromised people. Keep in mind that children are immune-compromised people (especially toddlers and children recently immunized).

Commercially prepared raw food diets for pets are readily available from holistic veterinarians and pet supply stores.

Some people will buy raw ground meat at the supermarket and make their own food. Store-bought ground meat is notorious for being filled with pathogenic (disease-causing) bacteria because of the increased surface area of ground meat.

It is extremely important to consult with a veterinarian who has experience with raw food diets before attempting to make your own, as nutritional deficiencies can result.

Important points to remember when considering feeding a raw food diet:

- Don't trust everyone who sells a raw diet. A lot of knowledge and quality ingredients are needed to formulate a safe and nutritionally balanced food.

- Don't feed a raw diet made of ground raw beef or turkey that is not first frozen. Processed diets like Darwin's are frozen, which kills most of the pathogenic bacteria. Some prepared raw diets are also irradiated.

- Be aware that veterinarians do see gastrointestinal (GI) illness secondary to raw diets. Other possibilities for problems are bones stuck in teeth, causing severe dental disease, as well as diarrhea and vomiting when some animals switch to a raw diet.

Homemade Diets

More and more people are learning to make delicious and nutritionally complete homemade food for their pets. Not only can homemade diets supply a pet with all the nutrients it needs, but many people also enjoy the feeling that preparing this food is a way for sharing their love for their pets.

A homemade diet does not simply mean feeding your pet what you eat, even if it is healthy food. You must take care to include all the necessary ingredients and in the right proportions. Deficiencies or excesses in ingredients can result in serious heath issues.

The resource section of this book contains information on homemade diets, but your best source of information is to discuss these diets with a veterinarian who has experience with them.

How to Feed Your Pet

Some veterinarians and nutritionists recommend meal feeding—offering a specific amount of food at a specific time. Food is put down for twenty to forty-five minutes twice daily.

Some of the benefits of meal feeding:

- Calorie control

- It is a more natural way for cats and dogs to eat.

- Knowing the diabetic pet has eaten before being given insulin

- Food becomes a reward after an injection or medicating.

- Decreased frequency of constipation

Others veterinarians may recommend free feeding—food being accessible throughout the day and night.

Some of the benefits of free feeding:

- Avoiding aggression between pets awaiting food. (This can be solved by quickly putting food out, having several feet between bowls, and making sure each pet has its own bowl or plate.)

- Convenience for owner

꙳ Some pets like to nibble throughout the day.

꙳ Diabetic pets have access to food when their blood sugar may be low.

Transitioning Your Pet to a New Food

Cats, especially, may develop an aversion to foods offered when they are not feeling well. If you are trying to switch your pets to a new diet, do it gradually and at a time when they are in good health.

Introduce any new foods gradually, and never switch an animal's food abruptly. It has been stated that cats will literally starve before they will eat a food they do not like. Never think that they should "tough it out" and will eat when they are hungry. In cats, not eating for as little as forty-eight hours can cause a serious liver disease called *hepatic lipidosis,* or fatty liver disease. When an animal does not eat for a period of time, its body starts to break down stored fat to use as a source of energy. This fat accumulates in the liver and causes the liver to shut down, resulting in the animal having no appetite. In order to save its life, the animal must get food into its system. The most efficient way of doing this is to have a feeding tube placed. (See Chapter 7 for more information on feeding tubes.) This is something that should be avoided whenever possible!

Basic steps for transitioning a pet to a new food:

Day 1: Mix 75 percent regular food with 25 percent new food

Day 2: Mix 75 percent regular food with 25 percent new food

Day 3: Mix 50 percent regular food with 50 percent new food

Day 4: Mix 50 percent regular food with 50 percent new food

Day 5: Mix 25 percent regular food with 75 percent new food

Day 6: Mix 25 percent regular food with 75 percent new food

Day 7: Serve 100 percent new food

For some cats, this transition needs to be extended to three to twelve weeks to be successful, especially if a cat has only eaten one type or brand of food its whole life.

The best way to tell if your pet is adjusting well to its new diet is to observe its stool. Runny stool, with or without blood or mucus, or both, is a sign your pet is not digesting its food well. Also be alert to any vomiting. You may have to go slower in your transitioning. If diarrhea lasts more than a day or your pet has vomited more than three times in one day, consult with your veterinarian.

Encouraging Your Pet to Eat

There are many reasons a pet may refuse to eat. Animals that cannot smell their food due to nasal congestion often will refuse to eat. Before offering them food, gently clean their nostrils with a warm, damp cotton ball, gauze square, or tissue. Warming the food will also make it easier to smell, and this may help greatly to improve their appetites.

Animals can have different preferences for the texture of their food. Some animals like chunky food, while others will only eat smooth (pate-type) foods. These preferences may change as they age or during times of illness. Offer your pet a variety of textures to see what may appeal to it. Pureeing food may also make it easier for your pet to eat.

Putting small pieces or a little dollop of food on a pet's tongue may also help stimulate it to eat. You can also try "top dressing" a pet's regular diet with something from the list below.

The following foods can be used to stimulate a pet's appetite. In addition, treats should only be used as long as it takes for your pet to regain its normal appetite. If your pet does not eat or drink for more than a day or two, please contact your veterinarian!

- Warm cooked or rotisserie chicken with broth (dark meat has more flavor and nutrients)

- Cooked and mashed chicken livers or giblets

- Stinky tuna, sardines, or mackerel

- Fancy Feast—various flavors

- Wellness canned foods, especially chicken and herring flavors

- Any brand canned turkey and giblets for cats

- Scrambled eggs with or without cheese

- Various types of dry food, including puppy and kitten dry food. Stay away from artificially colored and flavored dry food.

- Jarred baby food, meat-only flavors. (Check the label to make sure it does not contain onion powder, which may damage a cat's blood cells.)

- Rebound or CliniCare Canine/Feline Liquid Diet

- Dehydrated salmon, beef, or chicken treats, which can be crumbled on food or added to water to make a gravy

Nearly without exception, you should not feed a cat any food labeled for dogs, although it is fine to feed your dog some cat food to kick-start its appetite or to add flavor. Many dogs love canned cat food.

Some animals love the taste of nutritional yeast. Nutritional yeast has a nutty, almost cheesy flavor and is high in B vitamins. Sprinkle a little on your pets' food. They may really like it, and it's good for them in small amounts. You can find nutritional yeast in health food stores and bulk food sections of many supermarkets.

It you notice your pet sharply turning its head away from food when you offer it, it may be feeling nauseated. Other signs of nausea are drooling and lip smacking. Discuss these signs at once with your veterinarian. Medications can be prescribed to help curb nausea.

The following foods are very high in sodium and should be used in *very* small amounts for flavor only as a topping on your pet's regular diet. Note: Ask your veterinarian first if your pet has a heart condition and should not be given these foods even in small amounts.

- Smoked salmon

- Ham

- Deli meats

- Crumbled bacon

- Turkey or beef gravy poured on canned or dry food

- Parmesan cheese

Note: Warming foods and liquids increases the smell, making it yummier!

Often, a pet will sit in front of a bowl of food with no interest in eating until you put a taste of it on its tongue. The animal may not be able to smell it enough to create interest, but the taste on its tongue is all it needs to want to eat more. If you are not able to safely put it on your pet's tongue, smear a little bit on its nose or offer food on a spoon for it to lick off.

Aside from medical reasons, it is worth investigating if your pet is not eating for another reason. Have you changed the placement of the food bowls? Is another pet not allowing to it to eat? Is there something the animal is suddenly afraid of in the area it is being fed? Is the food too close to the litter box? Some pets are even picky about what they eat out of. Some animals prefer a flat dish, as they do not like when their whiskers are touching the plate.

Feeding an Emaciated Animal

Take caution when feeding an emaciated animal. While we all love to see a starving animal enjoy a meal, it is best to feed several small meals over the course of four to six hours to avoid potential serious consequences. *Refeeding syndrome* is a complicated series of physiological events that take place if too much food is given too quickly to a starving animal. Some of the signs of refeeding syndrome are muscle weakness and cramping, seizures, and respiratory problems.

Feed small meals of a commercial pet food diet that is high in fat and low in carbohydrates every four to six hours, and seek veterinary care as soon as possible. Have water readily available at all times.

Occasional vomiting or diarrhea, or both, are common in the first few days of feeding an emaciated animal. Bloody vomit or diarrhea is not normal.

Making Your Own Baby Food

Jarred baby foods can be quite expensive and often contain onion powder—an ingredient you want to avoid feeding your pet. Baby food can be made very easily at home and is much more economical. You can use cooked chicken, ham, or turkey. Cooked ground chicken, turkey, lamb, or beef can be also be used.

Note: Chicken and turkey breasts are higher in protein and lower in fat, while thighs and legs are higher in iron and fat.

Here is an easy recipe:

1 cup cooked boneless chicken, ham, or turkey, chopped into one-inch pieces

1/4 cup cooking juice (save the juices that you cooked the meat in) or plain water

Place the cooked meat in blender or food processor, and puree until a dry mix is formed. Slowly add water, and puree further until smooth.

Nutrition is an important part of keeping your pet healthy and happy. By learning all that you can about what to feed your pet, you will be helping your pet to live more healthfully.

⚜

CHAPTER 7

Assisted Feeding by Syringe or Tube

What you will learn in this chapter:

🐾 What syringe feeding is and how to do it

🐾 What some different types of feeding tubes are

🐾 How to feed your pet through a feeding tube

🐾 How to manage your pet's feeding tube and bandages

🐾 What some feeding tube complications are and when to call your veterinarian

There are many ways to encourage a pet to eat when it is just slightly off its food. (Please see Chapter 6.) But there are times when you need to be more proactive to ensure that your pet is getting proper nutrition. There are many reasons why an animal may not be able to have its nutritional needs met by eating on its own. Occasionally, in order to save an animal's life, feeding must be done by syringe or by the use of a feeding tube.

Syringe Feeding

Syringe feeding is delivering food via a syringe into an animal's mouth. Syringe feeding can be done on a temporary basis to get an animal through a period of decreased appetite or if dental procedures make eating painful.

There are different size and types of syringes. Small syringes hold 1 cc of liquid, while larger syringes can hold 60 to 100 ccs. Comfortable sizes for feeding kittens and tiny puppies are 3, 6, and 12 cc syringes. Feeding cats and other animals can be done with anywhere from a 12 cc to 60 cc syringe. Your veterinarian can supply you with syringes, or you can purchase them from a farm supply store, a medical supply store, or online.

For ease of cleaning and comfort in an animal's mouth, do not get syringes that have the luer lock on the barrel of the syringe. You can also use irrigation syringes with curved tips after cutting the tips off.

How to Syringe Feed

Choose a quiet place that is easy to clean. Syringe feeding can be messy, especially if you are doing it for the first time. Many animals will shake their heads, and food will fly. Put a large towel or blanket down that your pet can comfortably sit on. Small animals can be fed on a counter or tabletop, although many people like to sit on the floor and do this. Have on hand paper towels or small, damp washcloths for cleanup.

Prepare the food. Use a one-cup food processor, and process one five- or six-ounce can at a time. Adding a little warm water or broth can help liquefy the food so it can pass through the syringe. (You can also add a small amount of liquid diet, such as CliniCare, for extra calories and flavor.) This method enables you to use your pet's favorite chunky food if you process it long enough to make it smooth. Make it as smooth as possible because it can be very frustrating to have little bits clog up the end of the syringe!

Warm the food using one of several methods. You can microwave it for a few seconds at a time, but be **very** careful not to burn the food. Stir constantly to prevent hot spots in the food. A good method is to measure out the amount you want to feed, put it in a small bowl, and put that bowl in a larger bowl with hot water, stirring every few seconds until it is warm enough to feed. This takes a little longer, but there is not the danger of overheating. Another method is to place capped syringes of food in a pan of warm water. Make sure you don't let the water get chilly, therefore chilling the food. Test the temperature of the food on the inside of your wrist (as you would test baby formula) to make sure it is not too warm. Microwaving the food-filled syringes is not recommended, as you will not know how hot the food is inside the syringe.

Pull the liquid food into the syringe. Push out any air that may be in the syringe by pointing the syringe straight up and *slowly* pushing the air out. Delivering air into an animal's stomach may make it feel bloated and possibly cause gas. Wrap the syringe in a small towel to keep it warm while you go get your pet.

Bring your pet to the place you will feed it. Talk to it softly and calmly. It is good to tell your pet what you are attempting to do since they understand more than we think. Make feeding time a positive thing. Give yourself plenty of time for feeding, especially as your pet gets used to this new activity. You may only get a small amount of food into your pet at first, but this is better than frightening or stressing it. You do not want your pet to fear being fed. Keep in mind that for some animals, being restrained is very stressful, so find a way to do this gently and give them plenty of breaks. (Please see Chapter 10 for information on handling and restraint techniques.)

You may learn to feed your pet on your own, but at first, you may need another pair of hands to assist. If you are comfortable working on the floor, you can sit cross-legged with your small pet between your legs, facing away from you. You can also wrap your pet in a towel for gentle restraint. Choose a way that is most comfortable for you so you will not need to rush through the feeding process. Large dogs may need a gentle restraining hug to keep them in place when feeding.

Gently hold your pet's head and pull its lip up on one side with your thumb. Insert the syringe between its teeth, and angle the syringe toward the back of the throat. Some animals can really clench their teeth, making this very difficult. You may also try inserting the syringe in the front of the mouth. Press the plunger of the syringe slowly, and deposit a small amount of food in your pet's mouth. Delivering the food fast or in large quantities may cause your pet to choke. Make sure your pet swallows before you give more food this way. Your pet may need a break or to walk around a little as it gets used to this. Going slowly at first and having your pet accept this procedure will benefit everyone in the long run. Go slow when feeding to avoid your pet aspirating, or inhaling, the food into its lungs. This can cause a very serious problem. (See Chapter 9 for more information on giving liquids orally and to see a photo illustrating this technique.)

When you are finished, gently clean your pet's face with a damp washcloth if needed, and praise it for a job well done!

Contact your veterinarian if you are not getting the recommended amount of food into your pet or if it is vomiting.

Feeding Tubes

Placement of a feeding tube can help ensure that your pet gets the required amount of calories and necessary liquids. Most animals tolerate feeding tubes very well, and most people learn to manage them quite well. For more information on tube-feeding puppies and kittens, please see Chapter 14 for detailed instructions.

These are some of the more commonly used types of feeding tubes in veterinary medicine:

✥ Nasoesophageal tube (NE tube) or Nasogastric tube (NG tube)

These are common and relatively inexpensive types of tubes placed in cats and dogs for short-term use only. They are often placed after complicated or extensive abdominal surgeries. These tubes are fairly easy to insert with minimal sedation. A narrow, flexible tube is inserted into a nostril, fed over the back of the soft palate, and fed down into the esophagus (NE tube) or into the stomach (NG tube). The tube is taped and stitched into place on the animal's head. An E-collar is needed to prevent the animal from removing the tube. Some animals may sneeze the tube out, and care must be taken that an animal does not rub its face on things and dislodge it. NG or NE tubes cannot be used if there is facial trauma, if there is vomiting, if the esophagus is not properly functioning, or if the animal is not conscious. Because these tubes are very thin, they can become clogged, and only liquid food can be fed very slowly. It is best to use prepared foods such as CliniCare with this type of small-bore tube. These tubes can be kept in place up to one week.

 Esophagostomy tube (E-tube)

This type of feeding tube enters the esophagus from a small incision in the neck. Animals must be sedated or anesthetized for its placement. The tube is larger than a nasogastric tube, which allows for thicker food to be fed at a faster rate of delivery. This can also mean fewer complications due to fewer clogs. An animal will have a bandage wrap protecting the area where the tube is inserted. This area will need to be monitored and kept clean, which requires frequent bandage changes. These tubes can be kept in place and used for several weeks.

 Gastrostomy tube—PEG (percutaneous endogastric) tube

A gastrostomy tube is a large-diameter tube. Its placement requires short-term general anesthesia. It is surgically placed on the side of the animal and goes through the skin and the body wall, then directly into the stomach. An abdominal wrap is placed to protect the tube. The incision and wrap need to be monitored and kept clean, which requires frequent bandage changes. This type of tube can be kept in place and used for several weeks or several months.

Foods for Use with a Feeding Tube

A prescription diet may be recommended by your veterinarian, or you may be instructed to feed a high-quality canned food. These foods are liquidized to make them easily pass through a syringe and be fed to the pet via the feeding tube. Your veterinarian will instruct you, or you will need to calculate your pet's caloric needs for maintenance, weight gain, or weight loss so that you feed the correct amount.

Important rules for managing a feeding tube:

1. Only liquids should be administered through the tube. Small, chunky material can clog the end of a feeding tube. Medications in tablet form *must* be crushed and ground to a fine powder and mixed in liquid or food in order to be given via a feeding tube. A pill crusher or mortar and pestle work well. Take extreme caution when using powdered medications in NE/NG tubes in cats as there is a high likelihood it may lead to blockage.

2. Flush the tube with at least 5 to 10 mls of water (clean tap water is fine) before and after putting any food or liquid medication into the tube. The amount of the flush depends on the length of the tube. A large dog will have a much longer tube than a cat and require a larger flush.

3. Use a slow, steady pace when delivering food down the tube. Going too fast may cause nausea in a pet and possible vomiting. Do not be in a hurry! Based on how the pet is doing, start with about 5 to 10 mls at a time, taking a few minutes' break in between food administrations. Some pets can tolerate a faster rate; some need slower. If your pet smacks its lips or drools (suggesting nausea), you will need to go slower, feed a smaller amount, or take a longer break.

4. Liquids need to be a comfortable temperature, neither too hot nor too cold. Test the food as you would if feeding by syringe on

the inside of your wrist (as you would test baby formula) to make sure it is the correct temperature.

5. Keep opened cans of food in the refrigerator so they do not spoil.

6. Always keep the feeding tube capped when not in use or between times of delivering food into the tube.

7. If you notice any signs of discomfort, gagging, or coughing when putting the initial water flush into the tube, do not continue to feed. Contact your veterinarian for further instruction.

8. Discontinue feeding if there are signs of discomfort, restlessness, gagging, or vomiting during feeding. Do not attempt to feed again until the next scheduled feeding time.

9. Despite all good efforts and proper care, feeding tubes can occasionally get clogged. If you meet with a lot of pressure when trying to syringe water or food in, try flushing the tube with at least 5 to 10 mls of cola or plain 7Up soda. If this does not resolve the issue, please call your veterinarian.

10. Wash used syringes with warm soapy water. Push the soapy water out of the syringe as you would if you were feeding. This will dislodge any small bits of food that may be in the tip of the syringe. Rinse with water again, take the syringes apart, and dry them on a paper towel. After many uses, it may it become difficult to depress the plunger. If so, lubricate the rubber part of the plunger with a little olive or corn oil. Also check to make sure there is no obstruction in the tip of the tube.

11. Often, the tube will be marked with a pen line close to the insertion hole on your pet's body so that you will be able to gauge if the tube has changed position. If you think it has, contact your veterinarian at once.

12. If you have any questions about the feeding tube or the amount or type of food you are feeding or your pet's response to feeding this way, please contact your veterinarian.

Feeding Your Pet with a Feeding Tube

1. Follow steps 1 through 6 listed above.

2. Open any clamps and the feeding port on the tube. With a simple tube, you will just need to remove the plastic cap at the end. Slowly deliver the recommended amount of water to flush the tube. This amount is determined by the length of the tube. A tube placed in a large dog will need a much larger flush than a tube placed in a cat.

3. Slowly deliver the food through the tube, taking as much time as needed depending on your pet's tolerance and patience.

4. After the food is delivered, flush the tube again with a recommended amount of water. If necessary, wipe the end of the tube of any food with a clean gauze or paper towel. Replace the cap and close the clamps. Replace the outer bandage to cover the tube until the next feeding.

5. Rinse the syringes with warm and mildly soapy water, rinse well, take them apart, and allow them to dry on a paper towel.

6. Praise your pet for a job well done as it rests and digests its food!

Complications of Indwelling Feeding Tubes

Possible complications of feeding tubes include infection at the site where the tube has been inserted, accidental removal of the tube by pet or guardian, and clogging of the tube. Occasionally, an animal may not tolerate the tube for other reasons. Very infrequently, food will leak out of or around a gastrostomy tube and into the abdomen.

This rarely occurs because as the body heals, it creates an adhesion or stoma to prevent this. Incorrect placement of tubes is also a concern, and many veterinarians will take a radiograph (x-ray) to confirm that the tube is placed in the esophagus, as opposed to the trachea (windpipe).

Maintenance of Feeding Tube Bandages

Your veterinarian or veterinary technician will instruct you on the care of your pet's tube and bandages. You may be instructed to change the bandage daily or every few days. Have an assistant help you the first time you do this. Although the tube has been taped and sutured in, you must take care not to disrupt it.

How to change the bandage around a feeding tube:

- After removing the outer wrap and bandage material, check the tube position. (See above.)

- Check the insertion site for redness, swelling, and discharge. Note if the area seems painful to your pet. Normally, there may be a *thin* rim of pink or red tissue around the hole in which the tube is inserted.

- Clean the insertion site with an antiseptic solution supplied by your veterinarian. Gently clean crusts (debris) from around the tube with a warm, moist cotton ball or gauze.

- After cleaning, place a nonstick pad with antiseptic ointment around the insertion site.

- Cover the nonstick pad with several layers of gauze.

- Add a final wrap of bandaging material such as Vet Wrap® or CoFlex®. This will keep the bandage dry and clean as well as protect the feeding tube. Be careful when using these types of self-adhesive bandaging materials that they do not "roll up" and become constrictive.

Report the following to your veterinarian immediately:

- If the position of the tube has changed, feels loose, or falls out.

- If the area where the tube has been inserted and sutured looks red, swollen, irritated, or infected.

- If there is a foul smell, discharge, or bleeding around the site where the tube has been inserted.

- If any part of the tube looks torn or detached. Some tubes are very simple, while some have feeding ports, etc.

Intravenous (IV) Feeding

Animals with uncontrollable vomiting or unconsciousness may be fed through an intravenous (IV) line. This is not commonly done and is generally reserved for pets with a nonfunctional intestinal tract or who are not stable enough to undergo general anesthesia for placement of feeding tubes. Intravenous feeding of dogs and cats is complicated, difficult, and expensive. Feeding this way requires strict sterile measures and hospitalization. It is not the same thing as IV fluid administration.

Although tube-feeding can be very time-consuming and at times frustrating, it is often the best chance an animal will have to receive the nourishment it needs to save its life. The rewards are great when your pet makes it through this difficult time. And there is nothing like the feeling of seeing your pet eat on its own once the crisis has passed!

꩜

CHAPTER 8
Hydration and Water Consumption

What you will learn about in this chapter:

🐾 Why drinking water is so important for good health

🐾 How to calculate your pet's water needs

🐾 How to encourage your pet to drink more water

🐾 How to discourage water bowl spilling

🐾 How to get more moisture into your pet's diet

🐾 What dehydration is and how to recognize its signs

🐾 What subcutaneous (SC) fluids are and how to give them

The Importance of Water

Drinking enough fresh water is vitally important for us as well as our pets. Some of the functions of water are encouraging good digestion, flushing out toxins, supporting a healthy urinary system, helping to moderate body temperature, keeping skin and muscles flexible, and helping the body absorb nutrients. To help your pet's body carry out all these important functions and more, it is very important to encourage your pet to drink fresh water. And even if you never see your pet drink water, you must provide it at all times.

Calculating Your Pet's Water Needs

How much water your pet needs depends on its general health, age, size, and activity and stress levels. Pets living in very dry climates will require more water. Pets that eat fresh or canned food will require less water than pets eating only dry food. Fresh or canned food contains approximately 80 percent water, while dry food contains approximately 10 percent water.

Although these figures vary due to several factors, including your pet's health, here are some parameters:

ml = milliliter   kg = kilogram   d = day   lb = pound

๛ Normal water intake for cats and dogs is 20 to 70 ml/kg/d

๛ Normal urine output for cats and dogs is: 20 to 45 ml/kg/d

To figure this out, use the following example for a ten-pound cat:

10 pounds = 4.5 kilograms (kg)

(1 lb = 2.2 kg. Divide pounds by 2.2 to get the amount in kilograms.)

Using the middle range of 40 ml, we multiple 40 by 4.5 to get the amount of water intake per day: 40 x 4.5 = 180 mls

1 ounce is about 30 ml. To convert to ounces, divide by 30.

180 ÷ 30 = 6

An average ten-pound cat needs about six ounces of water a day. Remember, this is just an estimate!

It is recommended that you feed more fresh or canned food as your pet ages.

Encouraging Your Pet to Drink More Water

If possible, cater to your pet's wishes for drinking water (except for drinking out of the toilet and freestanding water outside.)

- Provide plenty of cool, fresh water at all times. Keep in mind that some pets may like very cold water, while others may like water that is room temperature.

- Some communities add chlorine to the water supply, and this may smell too strong for your pet. Letting the water stand in an open container for a day will help with the odor. Filtered and spring water are good choices to use, as they may taste fresher. They also contain fewer particles for the kidneys to process. Distilled water is *not* a good choice, as it may actually flush needed minerals out of the body.

- Provide several types of drinking stations for your pet throughout the house as well as outside. Some pets do not like to drink where they eat, so provide separate bowls of water away from food. Make sure that water is easily accessible at all hours of the day for elderly or mobility-impaired pets and that water is in places that are easy to see when the house is dark at night.

- Many a pet will appreciate its own glass of water on the night table. (Use caution and plastic cups, as some animals have been known to knock over glasses in the middle of the night!) One client of mine even has two cups on her night table. Both are plastic, but hers has a lid and straw. Now she and her cat are both happy!

- One of my clients got her dog to drink more by floating his favorite treats in the water bowl while he was watching. It became a game for him to get them out, in the process he ingested more water!

- Along with bowls of water throughout the house, another client puts a few inches of clean water in her bathroom sink every morning for her cat. Just make sure you do not use chemical-based ceramic cleaners if you are going to do this.

- It is also very important to make sure the water bowl is kept clean. Even if the bowl looks clean as you top it off with water, a slimy feel comes from dirt and bacteria. Washing water bowls daily with hot soapy water is highly recommended. Making sure you rinse them very thoroughly is also a must.

- Many cats and dogs like to drink fresh running water. As a result, there are now several different types of water fountains for pets on the market. See the resource section in the back of this book. Some pets, especially cats, can be suspicious of new things, so make sure you know they are drinking out of the fountain before removing the other water bowls.

Note: Many pets will readily use a water fountain right from the start. But for the suspicious ones, here are some tricks:

- Place it a few feet from the existing water bowl. Fill it with water but do not turn it on for a few days. Let your pet get used to this new addition to its environment.

- Leave a few treats or catnip next to it so your pet gets comfortable approaching it.

- Leave a trail of treats or catnip leading to the fountain.

- You can grow greens for your pet right next to it. This may help attract it to the fountain.

Discouraging Water Bowl Spilling

Do you ever wonder why your pet is splashing in or tipping over its water bowl? One theory is that pets may not be able to judge the distance from their mouths to the water, and rather than get a snout full of water, they test out how far away it is with their paws. Another school of thought is that pets like fresh running water and by splashing in it or tipping over the bowl, they are creating moving water. Yet another theory is that some cats do not like to get their whiskers wet. You may notice some pets dipping their paws in the water and licking it off!

Here are some tips that may be helpful:

- Use a spill-proof bowl made for puppies.

- Take a heavy ceramic water bowl. Place it in a shallow plastic tub with a piece of nonskid shelf liner under the bowl. For serious tippers and pawers, you may need to put a piece of nonskid shelf liner between the tub and the floor.

- Float a clean ping-pong ball in the water so the pet can judge the water level. Use caution that this does not become a choking hazard if you have dogs in the house that will want to play with a small ball.

- Try different types of bowls; some cats and dogs prefer a really wide bowl or have a preference for glass, ceramic, or stainless steel. Those that don't like wet whiskers may appreciate a narrower bowl with water filled to the very top.

Ways of Getting More Moisture into Your Pet

- Encourage water consumption. See above.

- Offer low-sodium beef, chicken, or vegetable broth, or tuna water to supplement your pet's fresh water. If you are going to serve your pet broth or soup, read the list of ingredients carefully. Onion in any form causes changes to certain blood cells and can cause illness or even death. Do not give soup or broth to your pet if it contains onion powder or onion salt. In addition, please ask your veterinarian if sodium needs to be restricted.

- Add warm water, tuna juice, or broth to your pet's food.

- Offer Rebound OES (oral electrolyte solution) a ready to use chicken flavored liquid containing electrolytes. This can be given to cats and dogs.

- Offer flavored water made especially for pets, or dilute an electrolyte-containing sports drink. *Do not use a sports drink if it contains xylitol, an artificial sweetener, as it is highly poisonous to pets!* Some pets like the sweet taste. You can freeze the sports drink in ice cube trays and offer a few at a time.

- Offer CatSip or a similar lactose-free cat drink.

- Offer your pet some ice chips to lick or crunch on.

- Carry a collapsible bowl and bottle of water when you travel with your pet. Offer it water frequently in warm weather.

Dehydration

Dehydration can cause serious problems in pets, especially if left un-treated. Problems can arise more quickly and be worse in the warmer months of the year and in warm climates. However, dehydration is a condition that must be considered all year long, especially in young, elderly, pregnant, nursing, ill, injured, and working pets.

Periods of uncontrolled vomiting or diarrhea, or both, can cause a pet to become dehydrated.

On a temporary basis, unflavored children's electrolyte solution can be offered to pets directly or mixed into food. *Do not use flavored solutions, as some artificial sweeteners can be deadly to pets.* As noted above, the ingredient xylitol is highly poisonous!

Do not replace your pet's water with this solution, as some pets will not drink it. This solution can be given by mouth using a syringe or turkey baster as long as the pet is not vomiting. Giving an electrolyte solution by mouth is not a replacement for veterinary care for an animal that is severely dehydrated for any reason. Go slowly whenever giving liquids by mouth so your pet does not aspirate the fluid, getting the fluid in its lungs by inhaling rather than swallowing the liquid.

Signs of dehydration:

- Lethargy

- Sunken look around the eyes

- Loss of appetite

- Skin that stays tented. You can test this by pulling up on the skin roughly between the shoulder blades. A well-hydrated animal will have skin that springs back with good elasticity. Note: This is not a foolproof test due to the differences in the types and amounts of skin a pet will have. One veterinarian who works exclusively with cats recommends pinching the skin behind the shoulder blades (toward the tail end) rather than between them in order to get a better sense of the cat's hydration.

- Dry mouth

- Gums that feel tacky. If your pet allows, gently press a finger on its gums. The gums of a well-hydrated animal will feel smooth and slippery. Gum color should quickly return to pink after being pressed with your finger. Note: Some dogs that are nauseated will have moderate drooling, and their gums may feel slimy even when they are dehydrated.

If you think your pet is dehydrated, seek medical care as soon as possible! Do not attempt to treat this on your own.

Giving Subcutaneous Fluids

At some point, your veterinarian may recommend giving subcutaneous (SC) injections of saline solution under the skin to support hydration, which in turn helps a pet feel better. SC fluids are not given in large enough volumes to achieve true diuresis. Diuresis is, simply put, the giving of large amounts of fluids to produce large amounts of urine that flush out toxins. True diuresis can only be achieved by giving IV (intravenous) fluids in higher volumes than are given under the skin.

The giving of SC fluids is commonly done, and a trained veterinary technician can show you how to administer the fluids if you do choose to do this at home. Many a cat appreciates in-home fluid administration, eliminating the need to be packed up and taken into the office.

Normal saline solution (NaCl) and lactated ringers solution (LRS) are commonly prescribed types of fluids for in-home use.

Low potassium levels (hypokalemia) can be an issue with some pets. For this reason, some veterinarians will add potassium (KCl) to the fluid bag for additional benefit. Use caution with volumes given when KCl is in the bag. *An overdose could lead to cardiac arrest, if too much is given too quickly!*

Vitamin B may also be added to the fluids in case the animal is deficient in this vitamin due to poor appetite. Vitamin B can also help stimulate appetite.

Hints for giving your pet SC fluids:

- Even fluids kept at room temperature may feel chilly to your pet. Warm fluids, and the IV line, excluding needle, in warm water bath. See step 2 on the next page.

- If you suspect your pet has a low body temperature, do not give SC fluids as it may not be able to absorb them. Seek veterinary care at once.

- Choose a quiet, pleasant spot where your pet feels comfortable. Avoid noisy appliances and high-traffic areas. If your pet is very sensitive, avoid the area where it eats so it doesn't associate anything unpleasant with eating.

- Rescue Remedy and Five Flower Formula, mentioned earlier in the book, are blends of flower essences that are great for people and pets that are feeling nervous about giving or getting fluids. Also, the scent of lavender is known to produce a calming effect in people as well as pets. Try a few sprays in the air (away from your pet) or on the towel your pet is resting on.

- Spray a towel lightly with Feliway to encourage your cat to relax and be less anxious. See Chapter 1 for more information on Feliway.

- Remember that pets pick up on our feelings very easily. Remember to breathe deeply and try to relax as you are doing this. Enlisting the help of a supportive friend or partner can help make this go easier, especially the first few times.

- Talk to your pet in a reassuring, positive manner. Let your pet know that this is a good thing that will help it to be healthier. Tell your pet that you are doing this because you love them. Consider the whole experience an in-home spa treatment for your pet as opposed to a dreaded medical procedure!

- If your pet gets squirmy, let it readjust or even take a little time out. Holding your pet down or restraining it harder may make it (and you) more stressed.

- Give a yummy food treat and praise after each session. Try to make this a positive experience for your pet. Some pets will even eat a special treat during the treatment.

Steps for assembling the fluid setup and for giving fluids under the skin:

What you will need:

- ❧ A sterile one-liter (1000 ml) bag of fluids as obtained from your vet

- ❧ A sterile fluid line. This is also called an IV (intravenous) line or drip set. Fluids lines have one or more clamps that stop and start the flow of fluids. There are also several types of clamps. Roller clamps have a piece of plastic that is rolled upward to stop the flow of fluids and downward to start it. Pinch clamps work by pushing the tubing toward the narrow part of the clamp to stop the fluid and toward the wide part of the clamp to start the fluids.

- ❧ Sterile 18-gauge or 20-gauge needles. The length is usually one to one and a half inches.

- ❧ A place to hang the fluids or a willing tall person to hold them. Fluids can be hung from a door hinge, a clothes hanger on a door frame, an IV pole, a nail on the wall, etc.

Some people find that sticking a strip of tape down the side of the bag (vertically, near the hash marks) then drawing a line at the horizontal level of the water before and after administration can make it easier to monitor the volume administered.

1. Obtain the bag of fluids, the IV line, and a new needle. At this point, you will need to get things organized before you get your pet. You want to have the equipment ready to go so there is no fussing and making your pet wait. The fluid setup may come assembled for you, or you may have to do this yourself.

2. If it has not already been done, remove the bag of fluids from its protective outer bag. Warm the fluids by placing them in a very warm water bath for twenty to thirty minutes. Take care that the water does not turn chilly in the process. Do not use boiling water.

Every few minutes, remove the fluids from the water and rock them back and forth to mix the warmed and cool fluids in the bag. *Warming the fluids is very important to do each time you give them to your pet.* Even room temperature fluids will startle your pet and may cause it to squirm, try to get away, or come to fear the process.

3. If you are assembling a new bag, you will need to do the following. Remove the protective covering from the port in which you will put the IV line, but do not touch the port itself. Remove the protective covering from the pointed part of the IV line. Insert the pointed part into the port of the IV bag. Pay attention that you push this straight in, as it is possible to puncture the port if inserting the pointed end of the IV line at an angle.

4. Remove the protective cap from the other end of the IV line, making sure you do not touch it or have it touch anything. Without touching the end of the IV line, run the fluid over your wrist so you can feel the temperature and to run any small bubbles out. It should feel warm. If the fluids feel cool, recap and repeat Step 2.

5. Attach a new and sterile needle, again making sure to keep the end of the IV line and the needle hub from touching anything. Some IV lines have a needle guard. This is a little cuff of plastic that screws up over the needle hub to prevent the needle and its cap from being pulled off together. You may need to experiment with needle sizes. An 18-gauge needle is larger than a 20-gauge needle. The fluids will flow quicker into your pet when using an 18-gauge needle. Most cats and small dogs easily tolerate an 18-gauge needle.

6. Hang the bag up high in a place where you want to give the fluids. Make sure the bag is facing toward you so you can see the lines on the bag. You will need to see them in order to know what amount you are giving. You may want to hang the fluids near a countertop, a chair, or a pad on the floor where you will place your pet. Some people like to hold small pets on their laps. *Remember, the greater the distance between the fluid bag and the pet, the quicker the fluids will flow.* Sitting on the floor with your

pet is a good way to do this, if you are comfortable. Some cats like to sit in small boxes when getting their fluids.

7. Bring your pet into the area and talk to it in a cheerful voice. See tips above. You may want to have some treats next to you for distraction.

8. Make sure all the clamps are open except for the one clamp closest to your pet. This will make it easier when it comes time to start the flow of the fluids.

9. Make a tent with the skin roughly between the shoulder blades. Using a quick and confident motion, insert the needle slightly downward at an approximate 30-degree angle (but with the beveled side of the needle up) into this tent of skin. There is no need to sterilize the skin. By using a confident motion, it will not only be easier to insert the needle but your pet will not feel your uncertainty and hesitation. You may want to make a clicking sound when inserting the needle to distract your pet as well as yourself, especially if either of you are feeling a little nervous.

10. Once the needle is inserted under the skin, open the closest clamp to start the flow of fluids. Even when not clamped, the tubing can remain crimped, therefore preventing the fluids from flowing. You can straighten the tubing by gently rubbing it between your fingers. Many animals will squirm a little as the fluids start to flow but then settle down nicely. If you notice the fluids flowing down your pet's fur, this means that the needle is not correctly placed under the skin. With some very elderly and dehydrated animals, it can be a challenge at first to place the needle correctly. This hap-pens to all of us, even after years and years of doing this procedure! Do not fret, replace the needle with a new one, and repeat Step 9

    Note: To see how fast the fluids are running in, look at the drip chamber. What you want to see is a solid column of fluid running. You may not always see this; you may also see drops. If the fluid chamber is full, you will not see any fluid running in, although it may be running just fine. To fix this: when the fluids are turned off, carefully turn the bag upside down and squeeze some of the fluid in the chamber back into the fluid bag.

11. Once the fluids are flowing, watch the bag to make sure you administer the prescribed amount. The first few times, you may not be able to give the entire prescribed amount but try to work up to the amount that needs to be given. Once you have given the correct amount, shut off one of the clamps, pinch the skin around the needle, and, taking care not to poke yourself, pull the needle straight out. Pinching the skin for twenty to thirty seconds helps to seal the tiny hole created by the needle. You may also want to have a tissue on hand to dry any drips of fluid on your pet's fur. Cats especially will appreciate this.

12. After giving fluids, recap the needle, and immediately replace the old needle with a new one. That way you don't have to re-member if it's a new needle or not next time! (Also, it helps keep bacteria from forming in the IV line.) Do not let the end of the IV line be without a needle or the cap the IV line came with. It is actually safer (for you) not to recap the needle after use but to dispose of the whole thing immediately in an approved sharps container for used needles. See Chapter 9 for more information on disposing used needle and sharps containers.

13. Store the fluids in a warm, dry place. If vitamin B has been added to the fluid bag, it must be kept in a dark place. Fluids should not be refrigerated.

14. Give yourself and your pet plenty of praise and a few treats for a job well done!

If the fluids aren't flowing, check or try the following:

- Make sure all the clamps are open and the tubing is not crimped.

- Reposition the needle by *very gently* changing its position under the skin.

- Lift up the skin above the needle gently.

- Move the fluid bag to a higher place.

- Turn the fluids off, and replace the needle with a new one.

Normal occurrences after giving fluids:

- Some fluid may leak out at the site where the needle was inserted. The fluid may be tinged with blood. There are no large blood vessels that you could have ruptured, but you may have disrupted a small blood vessel.

- Fluids may collect along one side of your pet or down a front leg due to gravity. This will be absorbed and not cause a problem.

- Your pet may lick at the area for a minute or two.

Always follow your veterinarian's instructions, and call him or her if you have any concerns about giving the fluids or your pet's general condition. Let the veterinarian know if:

- Your pet will not tolerate the procedure or is highly stressed by it.

- You are not able to give the amount of fluids prescribed.

- Your pet does not absorb the fluids within the time period the veterinarian recommends.

- Your pet's skin seems to bleed easily or form scabs. (This is very uncommon.)

- The fluids look cloudy, discolored, or if the date stamped on the bag is expired.

Most pets tolerate the administration of fluids remarkably well. Although you may feel uncomfortable giving them at first, this procedure can greatly enhance their quality of life. You can do this!

In the picture below I am sitting on the floor gently restraining Bumble in my lap. With my knees slightly upright Bumble feels cozy and comfortable and I can use both hands to administer the fluids. Many cats will tolerate this position allowing you to give fluids without assistance. If you are not comfortable in this position or your cat is not, placing them in a shallow basket or box (with a warm towel) can make them feel enclosed and less likely to try to run off.

CHAPTER 9
Medicating Your Pet

What you will learn in this chapter:

- What supplies should you have on hand

- What some medicating dos and don'ts are

- In what forms medications are available

- How to give a pill to a dog

- How to give a pill to a cat

- What a pill gun is

- What flavored medicated tabs are

- How to give liquid medication

- How to make a suspension

- How to easily administer a paste or gel

- How to administer eye medications

- How to administer ear medications

- How to use an inhaler on a cat or dog

◈ How to give a transdermal medication

◈ What the parts of a syringe are and how to handle and dispose of them

◈ How to give a subcutaneous injection

Medicating your pet can be as simple such as popping a pill in a piece of cheese and handing it to your dog. In other cases, however, you may have to resort to a highly sophisticated maneuver involving at least ten different flavors of canned food and the participation of the entire family when attempting to medicate your cat. But most times it will be somewhere in between.

When medicating your pet, relax and take a deep breath. Do not allow the process of medicating it to become a struggle. Your pet will remember it as a negative experience, and it will become increasingly difficult to give medication in the future. It is well worth taking the time to make medicating a positive experience, especially when it involves yummy treats.

Supplies to Have on Hand

◈ A selection of different-size syringes for administering medications and liquids. 1 cc syringes are small, and 60 cc syringes are large. In general, when giving liquids orally, a 3 cc syringe works well for cats and small dogs, and a 6 or 12 cc syringe works well for dogs. Note: 1 cc is the same thing as 1 ml. Usually syringe sizes are described in ccs.

◈ A pill crusher—this is a handy little device that pulverizes pills or tablets, turning them into a powder. You can also crush medication between two spoons.

◈ A pill splitter—this will split a pill or tablet in half.

꙰ A pill organizer—these can be handy for a pet on multiple medications.

꙰ A pill gun, also called a pill popper or pusher. This is described later in the chapter.

Medicating Dos and Don'ts

By understanding some basic concepts, you will learn why it is important to do your very best when giving prescribed medications. Here are some important principles:

꙰ Only give medications that are prescribed for your pet. If the medication had been prescribed in the past, please check with your veterinarian to before you give it again.

꙰ Always give the prescribed dose so that your pet benefits from the medication. More is not always better, and not giving enough can result in your pet not receiving the therapeutic dose of the drug.

꙰ Always finish a course of prescribed medication, even if your pet is improving and appears better. Failing to finish may cause your pet to have a relapse or need more medication later. Never save a portion of a prescribed medication to be used at a later time.

꙰ Never use one pet's prescribed medication on another pet without your veterinarian's approval.

꙰ Report any adverse reactions or side effects to your veterinarian immediately, even if they are minor. Some reactions may be normal, while others may be red flags for larger problems.

꙰ If you are unsure how, when, or even why to give a medication, consult with your veterinarian.

✺ Ask your veterinarian about using medications or products that are slightly out of date. In some cases, using them may be OK, while in other cases, it may be harmful.

✺ Store medications as directed and out of excessive heat and sunlight. Failing to do so may reduce the effectiveness of the medication.

✺ Do not give a double dose of medication if you forget a dose. Give medication as directed:

  ✺ If directed to be given twice daily, give every twelve hours.

  ✺ If directed to be given three times a day, give every eight hours.

  ✺ If directed to be given four times a day, give every six hours.

✺ It may be difficult to stick to some schedules, but do your best.

✺ Always shake or mix liquid medications thoroughly.

✺ Some medications are more effective when given with food, while others are more effective when given on an empty stomach. Always follow your veterinarian's instructions concerning this.

✺ Your veterinarian may prescribe a medication to be filled at a human pharmacy. The dose prescribed may be higher than what is prescribed to a human. Always follow your veterinarian's instructions even if the pharmacist wants to change the dose. Humans, cats, and dogs can metabolize drugs differently. Your veterinarian is trained to know and prescribe the correct dose for your pet.

✺ When in doubt about any medications—ask questions!

Forms of Medications

- Oral—Medications that are given by mouth: pills, tablets, capsules, or liquid. Liquid medications can come in the form of solutions (the drug is dissolved in water) or suspensions (the drug is mixed in water). Solutions are usually clear, and suspensions are usually cloudy. Because suspensions have particles that settle to the bottom of the bottle, it is very important that you shake these well before giving them to your pet. This will ensure that you give your pet the correct dose of the drug each time.

- Injectable—Medications that are given with a sterile syringe and needle

- Transdermal—Medications that are given on the skin and are absorbed into the bloodstream. They may be in the form of a gel that is applied to the inner ear or contained in a patch that is applied by your veterinarian. (See below for more information.)

- Topical—Medications that are given and work on the skin. This includes ophthalmic drops and ointments.

- Inhalant—Medications that are delivered via an inhaler or "puffer"

- Rectal—Medications that are given in the rectum such as Valium (diazepam) for animals that are having seizures.

There are several pharmacies that compound medications for pets. Compounding is basically defined as preparing a unique or custom dosage form for a specific patient. This can mean taking a medication that is usually given orally and putting it in a form that is more easily given when rubbed onto the outer ear. This works well for some animals for whom taking oral medications is very stressful or who do not tolerate them when given orally. Compounding can also mean taking a medication that is typically given in pill form and preparing it in a liquid form, usually with a flavor added to make it palatable to cats and dogs.

In general, if a tablet is coated, it means that the medication is bitter or tastes bad. It is best not to crush these or add them to any food or liquid. When giving your pet one of these medications, you can coat the pill with butter or margarine to make it go down easier and to disguise the taste.

Often, the medication enclosed in capsules is bitter. If your pet bites into the capsule, it may get the bitter taste in its mouth and drool profusely. A pet may occasionally gag or vomit from this. It is best not to hide capsules in moist food as the capsule itself will break down from the moisture, and the food will smell and taste like the medication.

Some medications, such as tramadol and metronidazole, are very bitter. If you handle the pills and put them in a treat, you will transfer some of the bitterness onto the treat, and your pet most likely will not eat it. Use a spoon or tweezers to transfer the pill into the treat of your choice. Then use clean hands that have not touched the pill to offer the treat.

Always follow any oral tablet, capsule, or pill with a small amount of water from a syringe! People don't want to swallow medications dry, and neither do pets. Any of these forms of medications could get stuck in a pet's throat, causing discomfort and, in some cases, damage. A 3 cc or 6 cc syringe works well to deliver water this way.

Giving Pills to Dogs

Here are some foods in which you may be able to stick a pill. Dogs will usually gobble these up!

- Cube of hard cheese or blob of cream cheese

- A piece of lunch meat

- A blob of peanut butter

- A blob of canned cat food

- A blob of canned cheese food product

- A blob of meat baby food

- A piece of sausage or hot dog

- A piece of bacon

- A piece of string cheese

- A chunk of soft bread

- A Pill Pocket™. Pill Pockets are flavored doughy pockets in which a pill or capsule can be put. They are available for cats and dogs in different sizes and flavors, including a variety for pets with food allergies.

If your dog will eat any of the above in one gulp, it is fine to hide a capsule inside; they will gulp it down before it becomes bitter tasting.

1. Make sure you understand the dosing directions and the amount to be given.

2. Find a quiet place to give the medication. Try not to be in a hurry. Your dog will feel more relaxed if you do.

3. Have the water chaser ready in a syringe.

4. Coat the pill or capsule with a little butter, margarine, or olive oil to disguise the taste and make it slide down easier. Note: Coating the pill may make it a little slippery and hard to hold onto.

5. You may need assistance holding your dog still, at least for the first few times. Ask a friend or family member for assistance.

6. Hold the pill or capsule between your thumb and index finger. If you are right-handed, use your right hand for holding the pill and your left hand for holding the dog, and vice versa.

7. Using the hand that is not holding the pill, place your hand over the top of your dog's muzzle and tip its head back. This should cause the dog's mouth to open slightly. You can also use your index and pinkie fingers from the other hand to gently open the mouth, but do not put your fingers between your pet's teeth. (See picture.)

8. Place the pill or capsule toward the back of your pet's tongue.

9. Close your pet's mouth, and hold it closed as you return its head to a natural position.

10. If your pet does not immediately swallow the pill or capsule, you can stroke its throat or blow on its nose. Both of these actions should cause it to swallow. Giving a water chaser by syringe will also help with swallowing.

11. Some dogs are champs at hiding pills or capsules in their mouths and spitting them out later. Watch your pet until you are sure it has swallowed the pill. Offering a tasty snack

immediately after giving the medication can be a way of offering praise as well as washing down the pill that may still be in its mouth!

12. Tell your dog what a great job it has done, and give yourself a nice treat!

Giving Pills to Cats

Giving pills to cats can be difficult, but here are some tricks to make the procedure go a little easier.

Here are some ways to disguise a pill in food:

⚬ Hide it in a Pill Pocket, and offer it this way.

⚬ Hide it in a Pill Pocket, and bury it in some very tasty canned food.

⚬ Hide it in a Pill Pocket, and put it in a bowl with a few pieces of a kind of dry food or treats that your cat loves but usually doesn't get.

⚬ If it is not a bad-tasting pill, you can crush it and add it to a small amount of tuna water, chicken gravy, or some very yummy food. Keep in mind that what we consider bad tasting or not differs from your cat's opinion because humans and cats have very different taste buds. Often, anything different is highly suspect. Add it to a small amount of food, and watch to make sure your pet eats it. Once your cat has eaten that amount, you can give it the rest of its meal.

Here is another great idea for getting a cat to eat its pill in a Pill Pocket. You can place the pill in the pocket and lightly moisten the pocket. Then, bread the pocket with a powdered freeze-dried chicken treat. Freeze-dried treats come in salmon, beef, and turkey flavors. They can be fed in chunks, crumbled, powdered, or as a gravy when water is added. See the Resource section for more information.

You can make your own pill pocket by microwaving a moist treat for several seconds to soften it enough so you can put the pill inside.

If your cat is smart, as most are, it may eventually not fall for the old "hide the medication in food" trick. Here are steps to giving your cat a pill by mouth.

1. Make sure you understand the dosing directions and the amount to be given.

2. Find a quiet place to medicate your cat, and have the medication and its water chaser all ready and nearby. Try not to be in a hurry. Your cat will feel more relaxed if you do. Again, take a deep breath, and don't show your anxiety.

3. Coating the pill or capsule with a little butter, margarine, or olive oil will make it slide down easier and help to disguise the taste and smell. It also makes it a little slippery to hold onto, so just use a little!

4. You may need assistance. If you are doing this by yourself, you may find it easier to do with your cat in your lap or between your knees. (See photo.) Some people find it handy to wrap the cat in a towel or to make a "bib" using a heavy towel so it cannot scratch you or push your hand away.

5. Hold the pill or capsule between your thumb and index finger.

6. Put your hand over your cat's head with your thumb and middle finger on each side of its face. Tip its head back so its nose is pointing upward. (Use caution with elderly cats, as they may

have some arthritis in their necks and along their spines.) This motion will make the jaw open slightly.

7. Using the hand with the pill, use your middle finger to gently pull the lower jaw down. Do not place your fingers between your cat's teeth!

8. Quickly pop the pill toward the very back of the cat's throat, and close the cat's mouth. Return the cat's head to a natural position, but don't let go quite yet.

9. Rubbing the cat's nose or throat, blowing lightly on its nose, or putting a tiny bit of food on the cat's nose should stimulate it to swallow.

10. When you are finished, tell your cat what a darling angel it is, and give it a nice little treat.

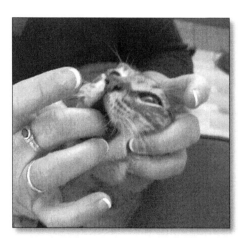

If all else fails, you can lightly hold the cat by the scruff, gently tipping its head back. This will cause the jaw to drop open. Then follow steps 7 through 9.

Pill Guns

Pill guns, also called pill poppers or pill pushers, are handy little devices used to pop a pill into the mouth of an animal. They are helpful for animals that bite or clench their jaws or for when you really don't want to put your fingers in a pet's mouth.

Some pill guns also have a water chamber that delivers the pill followed by a small amount of water.

To distract your cat or dog and to disguise the pill, put a blob of a favorite food on the tip of the pill gun after inserting the pill into the gun. If the pill gun does not have a water chamber, use a syringe of water after giving the pill.

Flavored Medicated Tabs for Cats and Dogs

Flavored tabs are a great way to get a cat or dog to take medication. These medicated tabs come in a variety of flavors for both cats and dogs and can be broken up and offered as a treat or crumbled on top of food. You may have a local compounding pharmacy that can make these, and there are several online pharmacies from which these can be ordered as well.

Giving Liquid Medications

When you are giving oral medications to your pet for the first time, it may be helpful to have someone else hold or gently restrain your pet while you administer the medication.

Read the prescription label, and make sure you understand the dosing instructions—how much and how often to give.

As some pets are masters at spitting out and flinging liquid medication everywhere, choose a place that is easily cleaned or place a towel down for your small pet. And remember, you do not have to have your pet's mouth wide open when giving liquid medications. In fact, doing so may mean the medication shoots right out the other side.

One veterinarian suggests getting your pet used to the syringe by placing a treat or yummy food on the syringe and letting it lick it off. This way, your pet begins to form a positive association with the syringe.

Steps for giving liquid medications:

1. Shake the medicine bottle if mixing is required before drawing the medication into the syringe or dropper.

2. Draw up the correct amount of medication into the syringe or dropper.

3. Hold the syringe or dropper in the hand that you normally use. Use the same position as in step 6 above.

4. Put the tip of the syringe or dropper in the side of the mouth, just behind one of the canine teeth. The canine teeth (in dogs and cats) are the large "fang" teeth. Most cats and dogs have two upper and two lower canine teeth. Push the syringe in so the tip is well inside your pet's mouth. Some pets will really clench their teeth, so you may need to wiggle it in.

5. Angle the syringe back and slightly to the side. Injecting the medication straight back into the throat may cause your pet to cough and inhale the medication. It will also make your job harder next time, as your pet may remember this as an unpleasant experience. You can also slowly squirt the liquid onto the roof of the mouth if your pet allows you to open its mouth wide.

6. Slowly push the plunger on the syringe to deliver the medication. Some animals will not give you the time to do this slowly, but resist the urge to shoot it in quickly for the same reasons as mentioned in step 5.

7. Rinse out the syringe thoroughly with water. If the medication needs to be refrigerated, do so now. Some people find it is helpful to keep the syringe on the medicine bottle using a rubber band.

Many animals, especially cats, will spit out some of the medication. Even if you are certain that your pet did not receive any of the medication, do not give more. Try again at the next scheduled dose. You do not want to overdose them.

How to Make a Suspension

Making your own suspension is easy and can be very helpful when giving a tiny pill, a part of a pill, or several tiny pills or parts of pills at once. It is easier to tell if you have gotten the medication into your pet when giving it this way, and it is much easier than giving two or three separate pills. Cats or any pet that is difficult to give pills to will especially appreciate this!

This method can also be used with the contents of a capsule, but medications are often contained in capsules for a reason. They almost always taste terrible! Some medications do not dissolve well in water, so oil (tuna, olive, etc.) may work better for some.

Bitter medications will still taste bitter using these methods, and your pet may act accordingly. Some medications dissolve readily while others do not. If in doubt, it is best not to waste a dose of medication. Coated medications will take longer to dissolve and most likely will have a bad taste.

Method #1

1. Crush the tablet or pill using a pill crusher or the back of a spoon, and put this in a very small and shallow bowl.

2. Add a small amount of liquid, broth, creamer, etc. The volume of liquid should be less than 2 ccs for cats and small dogs if possible.

3. Stir until the medication has dissolved, and draw it up into a syringe.

4. Administer as you would oral medication.

5. Rinse and reuse the syringe.

Method #2

1. Use a clean 3-cc syringe for cats and small dogs or a 6-cc or larger syringe for dogs.

2. Take the plunger out of the syringe, place the pill or tablet inside, and replace the plunger.

3. Draw up into the syringe a small amount of liquid, broth, creamer, etc.

4. Wait for the pill to dissolve. Slowly rock the syringe back and forth to mix and administer by mouth.

Giving Pastes or Gels by Syringe

Nutritional supplements and hair ball preparations often come in a sticky gel that is difficult to give. In the past, people were advised to put some on a pet's paw and it would lick it off. The reality was the pet more often flicked it off onto the wall and got it stuck in its fur. Here is an easier way to give pastes and gels.

1. Get a clean 3 cc syringe (for cats and small dogs) or a 6-cc syringe for dogs.

2. Remove the plunger from the syringe.

3. Hold the open end of the syringe barrel up to the tube opening, and gently squeeze the paste into the tube. Do not fill

the whole syringe barrel with the paste, as you will need space to re-place the plunger.

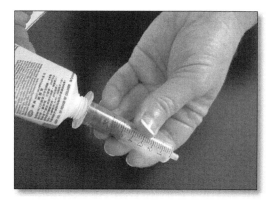

4. Slowly replace the plung-er, and administer the paste by mouth.

Slightly warming the tube of gel in warm water can make it easier to squeeze out, but be careful—warming it too much will make it very runny.

Administering (Instilling) Eye Medications

Eye medications will come in either a liquid form (drops) or as an ointment in a tube. In general, the eye is very efficient at cleaning itself by blinking and producing tears. These functions help to re-move foreign objects and substances. Because of this, medications put into the eye have a very short "contact time." This is why some eye medications are instructed to be given every few hours. Do your best to follow these instructions whenever you can.

Only use medications that have been dispensed by your veterinar-ian for use in the eye. Using an ointment or drops not meant to be used in the eye can result in damage to the eye and even blindness.

Never use eye medications that are expired. You can usually find the expiration date on the crimped part of the tube if you no longer have the original box or vial that the medication came in. Never use tubes of eye ointment if they have been punctured or damaged.

Wash your hands before administering any eye medications. It is also a good idea to wash after medicating to prevent possibly spread-ing infection. You may need to gently clean around your pet's eyes with a warm, damp washcloth or cotton ball before administering the eye drops or ointment.

Often, eye problems are painful, and it may be best to have help when medicating your pet's eyes for the first few times. Cats and small dogs can be gently held on your lap if you are administering the medication on your own. Larger dogs can be given a "snuggle" around the neck. See Chapter 10 for more information on gentle restraint techniques.

Steps for administering (instilling) eye medications:

1. Wash your hands.

2. Make sure you understand the instructions on the label.

3. Hold the bottle or tube between your thumb and index finger with the tip pointed downward.

4. Be careful not to let the tip touch anything, including your pet's eye. If this does happen, wipe the tip with a clean tissue.

5. With your other hand hold your pet's head. Your thumb can gently pull the fur across the top of the head; this will help to open the eyelids. The hand that is holding the tube or bottle rests gently on the side of your pet's head and pulls down slightly to further open the eyelids. (See photo below.) When holding the bottle or tube close to the eye, be very careful not to touch the surface of the eye.

6. Squeeze out the prescribed number of drops onto the eyeball, or squeeze a small ribbon of ointment across the eyeball. Release your hands, allowing your pet to blink. This will cause the ointment to melt and spread across the eye or the drops to be distributed over the surface of the eye.

7. If medicating both eyes, reposition your hands slightly to do the other eye.

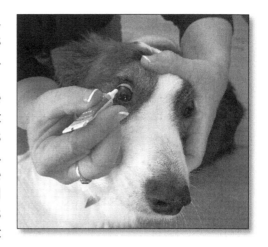

When using liquid drops, be careful not to squeeze out enough to run down the pet's face and get into its mouth. Some eye medications have an especially bitter taste, and your pet may remember this when you try to give the next dose.

After being medicated, some pets will blink and try to paw at their eyes; this is normal for a minute or two. If possible, do not let them paw at their eyes as this may cause further irritation or damage. Giving your pet a tasty treat or a toy may distract it as the medication sinks in. If redness and irritation worsen or if you believe your pet's eye is in more pain after you administer the eye medication, report this to your veterinarian immediately.

Instilling Ear Medications

Cats and dogs have ear canals that are shaped like an L. If you look into their ears, you will see many little folds and an opening that leads to the ear canal. The vertical portion of the ear canal is visible to us, while the horizontal portion is what your veterinarian can see with an instrument called an *otoscope*. At the end of the horizontal ear canal is the eardrum. In order for ear medication to be effective, it needs to get into the horizontal portion of the ear canal.

1. Clean the external (outer) ear with a moistened cotton ball, gauze square, or tissue. You can use water or cleaning solution as recommended by your veterinarian.

2. Gently pull the outer ear (ear flap) up and back so you can see the inner surface of the ear. Slowly instill the medication into the lowest opening of the ear canal. If you are instilling drops, squeeze out the prescribed number of drops close to the opening of the ear canal. If you are instilling ointment, insert the tip of the tube straight 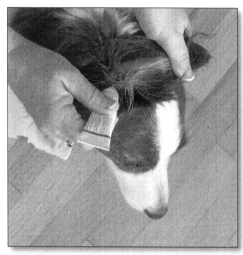 down into the opening, and squeeze out a small amount.

3. Massage the ear gently to distribute the medication deeper into the ear canal. You may hear a squishing sound as you massage the ear.

4. Stand back... Your pet now will most likely shake its head!

Using an Inhaler on a Cat or Dog

Metered-dose inhalers (MDIs) are used for treating inflammatory diseases of the respiratory tract such as asthma and bronchitis. Dogs and cats that suffer these diseases often benefit from inhalation therapy. When medication is inhaled, it is more efficient as it goes straight to the lungs as opposed to first having to travel to and be absorbed into the bloodstream. A delivered dose of this medication is often called a puff.

Most inhalation systems come in three parts: the mask or cone that goes over your pet's muzzle, the spacer that connects the mask and the inhaler, and the inhaler itself. The inhaler contains the medication.

Many animals may not be initially comfortable having the mask placed over their faces. You may need to work up to actually delivering the medication via the inhaler by using these easy steps:

1. Take only the mask and some tasty treats.

2. Gently place the mask over your pet's face and give it a few treats.

3. Repeat this a few times a day for as long as it takes for your pet to feel comfortable having the mask on its face. You may want to start out doing this for a few seconds and then build up to a longer time as it gets used to it.

4. When ready, connect the spacer and inhaler, and use as directed. Give more treats!

Steps for using the inhaler:

1. Have all your supplies ready. These include the inhaler, the spacer, and the mask. The system you use may be slightly different depending on the brand you use.

2. You will need to prime the system before the first use. Shake the inhaler, and follow the manufacturer's instructions to deliver a few puffs of the medication. Often, these first few puffs contain higher concentrations of the drug that is being delivered, so do not use the inhaler on your pet before this important first step.

3. Place the mask on the end of spacer.

4. Keeping the inhaler upright, attach the inhaler to the other end of the spacer.

5. Gently place the mask over the pet's muzzle, making a gentle seal around the nose and mouth. You may need assistance with this step if you have a very large or wiggly pet.

6. Dispense a puff of medication into the spacer by pressing down firmly on top of the metal canister. *Deliver only as many puffs as prescribed!*

7. The times will vary, so follow your veterinarian's instructions for how long your pet needs to breathe the drug through the mask. Often, this is measured in seconds or number of breaths your pet takes. Some inhalant systems have a flange or flap that you can see move as the pet takes a breath. You may be instructed to watch for this and count the movements. These movements indicate a breath being taken.

8. Always follow your veterinarian's instructions when using the inhaler. As always, if you have any questions about the process of medicating your pet or its medical condition, contact your veterinarian at once.

To help a pet relax while having the medication administered, try gently massaging their shoulders or lightly petting them.

Giving Transdermal Medications

Using transdermal formulations can be very helpful for a pet that is not easily medicated. Usually the inside of the ear (closer to the ear tip than the ear canal) is where these medications are applied. One of the downsides to transdermal medications is that the amount of drug actually absorbed into the bloodstream may vary. Occasionally, local irritation, allergic reactions, or hypersensitivity to the transdermal medication may occur.

These drugs have been formulated to cross the skin barrier, so it is very important that you wear protective gloves or wear a finger cot. This will prevent you from being exposed to and absorbing the actual drug.

Steps for applying a transdermal medication:

1. At least for the first few times, have an assistant gently hold your pet. It may be helpful to distract the pet with a treat or toy.

2. Find a spot on the inner ear that is clean, dry, and relatively free of hair. Discuss with your veterinarian the cleaning of your pet's ears beforehand or the possibility of shaving a little area if your pet has very furry ears.

3. Dispense the correct dose of medication onto your gloved fingertip.

4. Gently rub the medication into the skin using your gloved fingertip. Do not apply it so thickly that a blob of medication can fly off if your pet shakes its head after the medication is applied.

5. Some pets will need to be distracted from scratching or rubbing the ear after application. You can try feeding your pet, taking it out for a walk, or distracting it with a toy.

Some veterinarians will recommend alternating ears when medicating or will recommend cleaning the ears every few days. Do not clean your pet's ear immediately before administering the medication. Make sure your pet's ears are completely dry before applying any medication.

Some pets may be prescribed a transdermal medication patch. The pain-relieving drug fentanyl is often used in patches. Patches are applied at the veterinary hospital after a small area is shaved, usually on the pet's side. A protective wrap or bandage may be applied over the patch to prevent a pet from licking, chewing, or ingesting the patch. Serious side effects may result if a pet eats a patch. It is also important to make sure your pet does not lie on its side on a heating pad or surface, as this may cause increased absorption of the drug.

Giving Injections

Many people, not only caretakers of diabetic pets, can learn to give injections at home to their pets. The advantages to giving medication by injection are that you will know that your pet has actually received the medication, it can often be easier than giving medication by mouth, and for animals that are vomiting, there is no concern that they have vomited up the medication. A person's comfort level in giving injections can vary widely. Although the thought of giving injections can be scary, by working closely with your veterinarian or veterinary technician, even the most tentative pet guardian can learn the skills to do this correctly and with confidence. Since the needles used for injections are generally small, many animals hardly feel it when getting an injection. In general, injections of medication often do not sting the way vaccines do. For some pets, the worst part of the injection is being made to sit still!

Subcutaneous (under the skin) injections are given in loose skin, generally between the shoulder blades.

Some injections can and should be given in the muscle. Your veterinarian will give you instruction on intramuscular injections, as it is very important to do them correctly.

The Parts of a Syringe

A syringe has four parts: the syringe barrel, the plunger, the needle, and the needle guard (cap).

Syringes come in a variety of sizes from 0.25 ml to 450 mls, although syringes larger than 60 ml are rarely used with cats and dogs. The syringe barrel has lines (gradations) printed on it that indicate fractions of milliliters (ml). Syringes have these measurements printed on

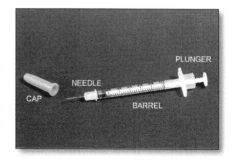

them to ensure a precise amount of medication or liquid is delivered when used correctly. Note: 'ml' is the abbreviation for milliliter, while 'cc' is the abbreviation for cubic centimeter. One milliliter is the same amount as one cubic centimeter.

Syringes are packed individually to keep them sterile. To ensure the sterility, keep the needle from touching anything before you inject your pet. Do not take the plunger all the way out of the syringe barrel, and do not let it touch anything.

Syringes are designed for single use only. It is not a good practice to reuse syringes. When syringes are reused:

- The needles become dull and are less comfortable to the pet getting the injection.

- It increases the possibility of introducing bacteria under your pet's skin as well as into the bottle of medication when you are drawing up another injection.

Often the injections that are prescribed from your veterinarian will already be drawn up into a syringe for you. If you are required to draw medication from a vial or bottle, have a member of your veterinary team show you how to do this and how to eliminate air bubbles in the syringe. This will ensure you are drawing up and injecting the proper dose. See photo for basic idea and position of how to do this.

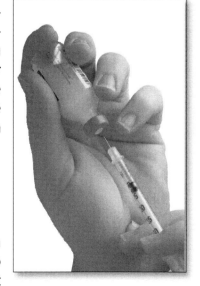

Steps for giving a subcutaneous injection

1. You may want to enlist the help of an assistant the first few times you do this, or you can try offering your pet

some especially yummy food or treat while you give the injection. This can be a wonderful distraction.

2. Make sure you have your injection close by. You may want to loosen the cap on the needle to make it a little easier.

3. Pinch the loose skin roughly between the shoulder blades, using your thumb and forefinger. This forms a tent.

4. Hold the syringe with your other hand in a way that is comfortable. It is helpful to practice your grip with a syringe without a needle prior to your first injection.

5. Using a quick and confident motion, insert the needle slightly downward at an approximate 30-degree angle (but with the beveled side of the needle up) into the tent of skin. Inserting the needle without hesitation will be more comfortable for your pet. You may notice it also makes it easier for yourself.

6. Some veterinarians recommend you pull back on the plunger of the syringe to make sure you do not have any blood in the syringe. This would indicate that the needle is inserted into a blood vessel. If you do notice blood in the syringe, discard the injection and start all over with a new syringe and medication.

7. Administer the contents of the syringe completely.

8. Once you have finished injecting, remove the needle and gently massage the area. Put the cap back on the needle to prevent accidentally sticking yourself or your pet.

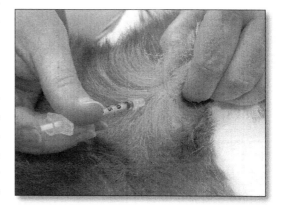

9. Give yourself and your pet a treat and praise for a job well done!

If you feel liquid on the skin after injecting, you may not have gotten the entire contents of the syringe under the skin. Unless advised by your veterinarian, do not give an additional injection until the next scheduled dose.

How to Handle and Dispose of Syringes

Even the most experienced person needs to take care when handling syringes with needles. Before you give injections, make sure you are comfortable handling the syringe. Veterinary technician students, before learning to give injections, are often instructed to practice by first holding the syringe without a needle. When comfortable with that, they practice drawing back with and pushing in the plunger, as if giving the injection. It may feel awkward at first, but with a little practice and repeating the maneuver, you can feel comfortable. It may be helpful for you to practice handling the syringe and injecting water into a piece of thin-skinned fruit, such as a plum. (If doing a practice injection on your pet, you will need to use a sterile liquid such as sterile saline solution. Do not inject tap water!) Just remember, even the most experienced veterinarians and technicians learned this very way. No one is born knowing how to give an injection!

Take caution not to accidentally stick yourself when replacing the cap on the syringe, and dispose of it in an appropriate container. Sharps containers are specifically made for collecting and disposing of used needles and syringes with needles. These are usually available from your veterinarian and pharmacy. Until you obtain one or if you will be returning the used syringes and needles to your veterinarian, any type of container (laundry detergent, mayonnaise jar, etc.) with a snug-fitting or screw-on lid can be used. Check with your veterinarian or local waste management company for policies and places to take filled containers. Local waste management companies can advise you on the acceptable way to store and where to dispose of used needles and syringes with needles if you are not using a sharps container.

Many will require the used needles and syringes with needles to be in a rigid red container and to be securely taped closed. Never put needles and syringes (even well wrapped) into your trash can.

While learning to medicate a pet can be stressful, by being creative and patient, you can find ways to do this successfully. With practice, you will be able medicate your pet with minimal stress for everyone.

✿

CHAPTER 10
Handling Techniques for Pets

What you will learn in this chapter:

✿ Stress and handling animals

✿ How to work with a challenging pet

✿ How to use an e-collar, muzzle, or harness

✿ What is an anxiety wrap

✿ How to restrain using the toweling method

✿ How to restrain a large, friendly dog

Stress and Handling Animals

It is the nature of animals to be self-protective when they perceive that they may be hurt. In addition, many animals are smart enough to know when a person is about to do something to them. This can be intensified when they are injured or feeling unwell. Even the most docile pet may put up a struggle when being medicated, treated, or having a procedure done. It is our job as guardians to make any procedure go as quickly and painlessly as possible so as to not cause further distress.

While it is not wise to rush through medicating or treating a pet, many will become suspicious if you are trying hard for any length of time to get them to come to you, especially if this happens several times a day or involves things that smell unfamiliar. Often, the best approach is to make medicating and treatment times low-key and to get them finished quickly. You may have to gently pick up or restrain your pet to get the job done. Unless the medicine is hidden in a wonderful treat that your pet can't resist, don't expect it to come right up to you! There are methods to use to gently restrain and handle a pet with the goals of everyone's safety and comfort in mind.

In general, unless an animal is showing signs of aggression (for whatever reason), less restraint is better. Most animals will react to being overly restrained by struggling more to get free. They may also try to bite or scratch. Would we not do the same thing if pinned down with the perception we were going to be hurt?

Pets can pick up on our feelings, and if we are nervous and unsure, they can sense this. They will often take advantage of that fact. It may be helpful to try to convey to your pet that you are doing something *with* them or *for* them as opposed to something *to* them. By adopting that attitude, you may feel more comfortable when you are doing something your pet may not enjoy.

In addition, if you are uncomfortable with seeing bandages being changed, injections or SC fluids being given, etc., and you are the person restraining, it is best to look away. Your anticipation of the needle or your discomfort at the sight of a wound could cause you to tense up, which in turn may cause the animal to react or pick up on your stress.

Talking to any animal, especially a frightened one, is very helpful. Talking in a quiet, soothing tone of voice can be very comforting. Avoid high-pitched tones, and keep the spirit of what you are saying positive.

It is best to not to try any kind of restraint if there are a lot of distractions happening around you, such as loud television or music, children running around, and general household chaos. It is much easier to work with an animal in a quiet, peaceful environment. In addition, do not rush when handling and treating your pet. A calm environment and handler will mean a calmer animal.

Many animals, especially cats, are more comfortable with all four feet on the floor. Others are more comfortable being held snugly next to you. Every animal is different, and you may need to try different techniques to see what your pet is most comfortable with.

Working with Challenging Pets

Some pets may be labeled as "fractious" or AWC (approach with caution) in the hospital. They may be challenging to handle even at home. Although much thought must be given to treating these animals, many people have found a way to work with their pets' difficult behavior. A lot of this behavior is caused when an animal is frightened of what you may be trying to do or not feeling well, or both. Working slowly and gently while reassuring your pet may lessen its fears.

Some animals may anxiously anticipate that you are going to medicate or do something else to them. They may show the following signs of fear when approached:

- They may have dilated pupils.

- They may have their ears pulled back.

- A dog may have its tail tucked.

- A cat may be swishing its tail.

- They may be growling or hissing.

- They may be looking nervously for an escape route.

Especially with a fearful animal, stand sideways or crouch down near it. Avoid standing right over the animal, and avoid direct eye contact. Avoid reaching right over the animal's head; instead reach under the chin (but be mindful if you think the pet may bite in fear.)

These techniques will make you appear smaller and less threatening. Offering a treat may also make your pet more comfortable.

When working with very fearful animals, remember that most fearful animals would rather flee than fight. It is also important to remember that a very fearful animal will bite or scratch if it feels cornered.

Using E-collars, Muzzles, and Harnesses

Working with confidence and good intentions can make the difference when dealing with a challenging situation. Using an e-collar or muzzle can help to give you the confidence needed to quickly and effectively treat your pet. Some people may immediately reject the idea of the use of a muzzle on their pets. But when the fear of being bitten is taken out of the equation, you will not be projecting fear onto your pet. Instead of fear, your pet will be more likely to pick up on your confident feelings. Using an e-collar or muzzle can also act as a distraction to a pet that is worried about what you are trying to do. While it is thinking about what is on its face, you may be able to quickly change a bandage, give an injection, or apply medication in an ear. In time, the collar or muzzle may not even be needed.

E-Collars: One friend of mine was afraid of being bitten by her beloved but rather aggressive cat. She still wanted to give him a chance at treatment for diabetes. Before giving the insulin injection, she would slip an e-collar on her cat. This enabled her to give the insulin injections quickly and without fear of being bitten. In time, the collar was no longer needed, as her cat learned that nothing bad was going to happen and that a tasty meal was given at the same time. Thor lived with diabetes for eight years and passed away at the age of nineteen.

See Chapter 1 for more information on e-collars.

Muzzles: The use of muzzles is always a topic of controversy. Perhaps using the term "nose mitten" will help the useful muzzle sound a bit friendlier. Muzzles can be made in different styles of plastic, leather, coated wire, and tear-resistant cloth. Along with the part that fits over the muzzle, the muzzle also has a strap that buckles behind the ears, and some also buckle over the head. Fabric muzzles for cats, sometimes called hoods, often use Velcro as a closure on the strap.

There are many sizes and styles of muzzles for dogs and several sizes for cats. It is very important never to use a muzzle on an animal that is having trouble breathing or is vomiting. Always use the appropriate style of muzzle so that the muzzle does not interfere with breathing. Because dogs and cats cool themselves by painting, do not use a muzzle on an overheated animal. *Never leave a muzzle on an unattended animal!*

Harnesses: A harness can make handling a very wiggly cat or dog more manageable. Aside from the fact that the harness will often act as a distraction, the harness will give you more control. Using a "walking jacket" type of harness can feel comfortable and reassuring to a cat or dog.

Anxiety Wraps, T-shirts, and "Thundershirts"

For centuries, the practice of swaddling has produced calm and happy babies. There are different theories on why this works, but now these practices have been adapted for use on nervous or fearful cats and dogs.

Some people will simply put a tight-fitting T-shirt on their dog. (Some cats will also tolerate this!) Others learn to make an anxiety wrap using an ACE bandage. There is also the ThunderShirt for cats and dogs. According to the website for ThunderWorks, the ThunderShirt's patented design is a pressure wrap that applies a gentle, constant pressure on a dog or cat's torso. It is a well-made product that is easy to use.

The Thundershirt has been widely known to help in situations such as storms, separation anxiety, travel, grooming, vet visits, etc. It may be just as useful for relieving anxiety when working with or nursing your ill or injured pet at home. See the resource section for more information on ThunderWorks.

Toweling

The same theories of why pressure works to relieve anxiety may apply to the "kitty burrito," or "purrito." It is a safe and effective way to gently restrain a cat or a small dog. Some people refer to the bundling of a pet in a towel as "toweling."

You can let your pet get used to the towel by having it sit on it and offering it a few treats. Do not be in a hurry, and give your pet time to get relaxed also.

There are several methods of making a kitty burrito. Both start with a thick towel.

Method #1

1. While working on the floor with the cat between your knees or with your cat on a table facing away from you, lay a towel over the cat's back.

2. Take one side of the towel, and pull it across the cat's chest.

3. Repeat with the other side.

If a cat is very wiggly, you can tuck the sides and the back of the towel under the cat, although this may make some cats struggle more. Remember, with the average cat, less restraint is better! When cleaning ears or doing something on an itchy cat, a loose burrito works better as it allows the cat to do what it must—scratch its ears, etc.—but allows you some control and protection from its claws.

Method # 2

- Place your cat on top of a towel, roughly in the middle of it, when it is in the same position as in the first method.

- One at a time, pull the sides of the towel up and over the cat, tucking them under the cat as you go.

There are many variations of this technique. It is quite possible to make up your own depending on what works best with your particular cat!

Towel Collars for Cats and Small Dogs

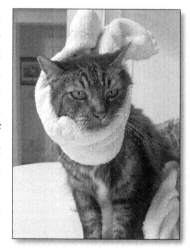

A favorite way to gently restrain a small animal is by making a thick collar from a medium-size towel. This works well for cats and small dogs that really mind being restrained and is a great alternative to "scruffing"- holding an animal tightly by the scruff of the neck. Towel collars work great when trimming nails, working with a pet's feet, grooming, etc. One person holds the towel while another works on the pet.

Steps for making a towel collar:

1. Fold a thick medium-size towel the long way.

2. Wrap it around the pet's neck with the ends of the towel facing toward the back of the pet. (See photo.)

3. Grasp the towel with one hand behind the pet's neck.

The animal is now unable to move forward, turn around and bite, or reach down and bite. The hand that is holding the towel is completely protected.

Restraining Medium and Large Dogs

The following method works well to restrain medium and large, friendly dogs. This can be done while crouching down next to or behind the dog. The advantage of restraining the dog from behind is that you can use your body as a backstop if the dog is wiggly or trying to back away from you. *This method should not be used with an aggressive dog as you may be putting yourself in an unsafe situation if the dog reacts quickly and tries to bite.*

Method # 1

1. With the dog standing, crouch down next to it on its right side and use your right arm to snuggle the dog under the neck.

2. Use your left arm to reach under the dog's abdomen just in front of its rear legs or over its back.

3. Gently pull the dog toward you.

4. You can also use your right hand to gently tickle the dog's face or the top of its head as a distraction.

Method # 2

1. Crouch behind a sitting dog with your knees on either side of the dog's body.

2. Use either your right or left arm to snuggle the dog's neck.

3. Drape the other arm across the dog's chest. This is useful when helping someone trim nails, change a bandage, or work with a dog's foot.

4. As above, you can also use your hand to gently tickle the dog's face or the top of its head as a distraction.

In the following picture I am restraining a medium size dog very gently but effectively. My hands are holding the paws that are closest to the floor and I am just slightly pulling them upward. This method works well with many dogs but caution should be taken and this should not be done on dogs that are very frightened or frantic at being restrained this way.

See Chapter 1 for information on Feliway, Comfort Zone for dogs, Rescue Remedy, and lavender spray. These are preparations that can also help pets to relax and be less anxious.

Contact your veterinarian if you are unable to safely medicate or treat your pet. Treating and medicating some animals can be a challenge. It is counterproductive if the process causes great stress to your pet, and care must be taken if it compromises your safety.

CHAPTER 11
Skin, Fur, and the Importance of Good Grooming

What you will learn in this chapter:

- Why having healthy and clean skin and fur is important

- How brushing and combing can be beneficial

- How to clip your pet's fur

- How to take care of incisions

- What aversive techniques are for stopping licking and chewing

- What abscesses are and how they form

- How to take good care of your pet's ears

- What anal glands are and when can they cause problems

- How to care for your pet's nails and feet

- When bathing is a good idea

- How to bathe a cat or kitten

- How to bathe a dog

- What waterless or dry shampoos are

❧ **What fleas, ticks, lice, maggots, and other nasty critters are**

❧ **What ringworm is**

As we all know, after days of illness or injury, it feels great to take a nice, hot shower or bath. Our furry companions feel just the same way—although they may not show their appreciation at the time! Good grooming is not only physically refreshing but also mentally refreshing. Have you ever observed a dog after a pleasant, cleansing bath or a cat that has had itchy and annoying mats clipped from its fur? Often, those animals will react by showing how good they feel and will prance around and look happy. I have heard many clients remark on how perky their cats became when freed from itchy and constraining mats. Not only does good hygiene make an animal feel good, but it is also important for good health.

Paying extra attention to a pet's hygiene is especially important for young, elderly, and frail animals. Many animals do a good job of taking care of these matters themselves, but some animals need extra care and attention paid to them to prevent potentially serious issues.

The Importance of Clean, Healthy Skin and Fur

Having clean fur and healthy skin is important for all animals. Healthy skin is a barrier and protects the body from infections.

When an animal is ill, it may not feel like grooming or be able to groom properly. There may be areas that it cannot reach. Often, hygiene becomes neglected, resulting in an unpleasant and unhealthy situation. Keeping the animal's coat and skin clean can make it feel more comfortable and avoid complications from irritated skin.

Prolonged contact with urine or feces when an animal is incontinent or unable to groom properly can cause irritated skin and sores. These sore can also become extremely painful and cause stress.

Cats and dogs with long coats may benefit from the fur being clipped under the tail, on the lower abdomen, and the "feathers" along the back legs. Keeping the hair short and clean will also keep these areas drier and prevent moist conditions that can breed germs and fungal infections.

In addition to under the tail, other places that can benefit from trimming are the ears, feet, and around the mouth, chin, and chest on longer-haired animals. Often, when an animal is being syringe-fed, these areas can get very sticky and matted. Elderly animals are prone to having mats in the hip area or under the front legs that can be uncomfortable and restrict movement.

Fur can be clipped by a groomer, in a veterinary office, or at home. Another option is that an experienced mobile groomer or vet tech can come to your home and provide these services.

Brushing and Combing

Brushing or combing your pet can be beneficial for many reasons. Brushing and combing help to keep the fur and skin clean and healthy by removing dead hair and skin cells, preventing tangles and knots, stimulating healthy oil gland production, and stimulating blood circulation.

Brushing can also help you locate painful areas. Many elderly pets are sensitive around the neck, spine, and hips. Brush very slowly and gently in these areas; avoid them if necessary.

Many pets find it pleasant and relaxing to be brushed. It can be an activity to which they look forward. Avoid sensitive areas and tugging on the fur when large mats or knots are present. (Sprinkling cornstarch onto a large mat can make it easier to pull apart or comb through.) Gentle brushing can alleviate stress that sometimes causes skin problems or outbreaks of allergic skin disease. It also helps you identify and monitor lumps and bumps that may arise. Along with any sensitive areas, please report these findings to your veterinarian. Some lumps and bumps can be benign or harmless, while others may need monitoring and possible treatment.

Brushing also helps alleviate hair balls. A severe buildup of hair balls can cause problems such as obstructions, ulcers, and impactions. Along with brushing, proper diets with healthy levels of fiber or hair ball preventative treats are recommended for long-haired pets, pets that over groom, and pets that have digestive issues. Ask your veterinarian for recommendations on what will work best with your pet.

Clipping Your Pet's Fur

Be careful when clipping, and do not clip the fur over skin that is already irritated or over open wounds. As skin and fur protect the body from infection, only clip the fur short enough so the area can be kept clean and dry. Clipping down to the skin (as in a surgical clip) is rarely necessary and may do more harm than good. Never use clippers that have broken blades with missing teeth, as these can tear and damage the skin. After every use, clippers should be cleaned, disinfected, and lubricated to keep them in good working order. Be especially careful with sanitation when you are using clippers to clip areas such as under the tail as well as using them on other areas of the body.

Never be tempted to remove a mat with scissors unless it is very far away from the skin. There are many affordable battery operated or electrical clippers on the market for use on animals. They are well worth the investment.

Caring for incisions

Sutures, also called stitches, are used to properly close wounds. After some surgeries, layers of sutures are used. Below-the-skin-layer absorbable sutures are routinely used and do not need to be removed.

The surface (skin layer) of your pet's incision may be closed with surgical glue, sutures, or surgical staples.

The edges of the incision should be touching each other, and the skin may be its normal color or slightly pink or reddish. Often, the incision becomes slightly redder following surgery. A few days after the surgery, slight bruising may also be noticeable, and this is also normal.

Please follow these general guidelines to ensure your pet will have uneventful healing. The directions may be slightly different depending on where your pet's incision is.

- Keep your pet indoors for seven to ten days to give the incision a chance to heal. Dogs may be walked with a leash.

- Restrict your pet's activity for seven to ten days.

- Do not let your pet be overly active, such as running, jumping, or leaping. Failure to do this can cause an incision to open up and resume bleeding.

- Do not bathe your pet or let the incision get wet.

- Do not let your pet excessively lick or scratch at the incision.

- Do not clean the incision with anything unless instructed by your veterinarian. This means no alcohol or hydrogen peroxide.

- Do not apply cream or ointment to the incision unless instructed by your veterinarian.

Call your veterinarian if you notice any of the following:

- Swelling, extreme redness, or skin that is very warm to the touch around the incision.

- Blood that is seeping from the incision for more than twenty-four hours.

- Foul-smelling discharge from the incision.

- If you cannot get your pet to stop licking or scratching the incision.

You may need to have your pet wear an Elizabethan collar, also known as an e-collar. See Chapter 1.

Aversive Techniques for Stopping Licking and Chewing

Many animals will lick, chew, and bite at incisions, wounds, and bandages. To deter a pet from disturbing the area, aversives can be used on the bandage or *around* the incision or wound, if an e-collar is not available or tolerated. Do not use any of these preparations *in* the wound. You can use:

- Commercial products such as Bitter Yuk! No Chew™ spray. This product does not contain alcohol and does not sting.

- PetFlex™ No Chew Bandage, a cohesive flexible bandage embedded with a bitter substance. This bandage does not stick to fur or skin.

- Diluted pepper sauce and water in a spray bottle.

Giving your pet plenty of attention and providing it with appropriate things to chew may help it from becoming bored and chewing on its bandage. Some animals, mostly cats, just can't stand having a bandage on and will try to remove it no matter what you do. Monitor your pet, especially if it is known to chew on objects or itself. You may need to place an e-collar on your pet, especially if it will be left alone for any length of time, especially overnight.

Abscesses

An abscess is a pocket of pus and blood that forms under the skin after an animal has received a puncture wound. This can be the result of a fight when an animal has been bitten or clawed. It can also happen after foreign material such as a thorn, foxtail, or splinter is poked through the skin. Bacteria are introduced into the wound, but the skin heals. This seals the bacteria in an environment perfect for infection to flourish. Cats are especially good at forming abscesses, as their bodies are very efficient at walling off infection. Common places for abscesses include the tail, side of the face, and paws.

Often, you will not know that your pet has an abscess until days later. You may notice your pet is hiding, acting lethargic, or will not eat. It may be grumpy and not want to be touched. It will often run a fever. By closely examining your pet, you may notice a swelling. The swelling may feel hard at first, and then soften as the abscess forms. It may continue to get larger until it opens and drains on its own. When it opens and begins to drain, an animal will start to feel much better.

Often, an abscess will need veterinary intervention. Sometimes a piece of rubber tubing will need to be placed so that the wound can continue to drain. Antibiotics may be prescribed in some cases to promote healing.

When an abscess is about to burst, you may notice a dark and bruised-looking area on the swelling. Other times, you will just see a wound draining with pus or blood, or both. Often, there is a very foul smell.

See Chapter 16 for how to treat an abscess if your pet is otherwise doing well.

Caring for Your Pet's Ears

Many long-eared dogs, such as spaniels and hounds, often have outer ears that can trap dirt, moisture, wax, and ear mites, all of which provide an excellent breeding ground for bacteria, fungus, and infection. To a lesser degree, cats may have similar issues.

Signs of ear infections include:

- Ears that are hot, red, or have a bad or yeasty smell

- An animal is constantly shaking its head, rubbing its head on the carpet, or scratching its ears

- There are scabs and fur missing from the base of the ears

Your veterinarian will look for what is causing these signs. He or she may choose to do testing and follow up with medications or treatments if necessary. You can help prevent these issues by keep your pet's ears clean and dry and using your nose to sniff out any potential problems!

If you think that your pet has an ear infection, do not be tempted to treat it yourself. By cleaning or putting any solution in the ears, you may be doing more harm than good. You may push the infection deeper into the ear, accidently rupture the eardrum (tympanic membrane), and make it harder for your veterinarian to identify the bacteria or fungus causing the problem. In addition, using a cleanser in an ear canal with a damaged eardrum could cause deafness. If you have any doubt, have your veterinarian examine your pet's ears to make sure they are healthy and can accept cleanser to remove waxy debris.

Dr. Trish Ashley of Veterinary Allergy and Dermatology in Springfield, Oregon, recommends that pet guardians "fill ear canals with cleaning solution. Massage canal for fifteen seconds then let them shake their head. Clean debris that comes to the opening of the canal. We do not recommend that clients use Q-tips at all."

See Chapter 9 for how to medicate your pet's ears.

Anal Glands

Cats and dogs, along with many other carnivorous mammals, have two anal sacs, also known as anal glands. They are located at roughly the four o'clock and eight o'clock positions on a pet's anus. Each anal gland has an opening to the outside of the pet's body. These glands contain a very foul smelling liquid that is expressed, or forced out, when an animal has a firm bowel movement. When the fluid isn't expressed, it can build up inside the gland or glands. This can be very painful and cause the glands to abscess and burst. Cats, to a lesser degree, also have a problem with anal glands. To avoid problems, many people will routinely have their dogs' anal glands manually expressed, usually by a veterinary technician or groomer. Some people choose to learn how to do this procedure at home.

Signs of anal gland problems:

- A pet that is scooting or dragging its backside along the floor or carpet.

- A pet that is licking or chewing at the area above or below its tail.

- Redness, thickening, or a swollen area near the pet's anus

- Blood or pus draining from the area near the pet's anus

- A pet that cries out or reacts strongly when defecating

- A pet that is reluctant to sit down

Nail and Foot Care

Healthy, mobile animals will naturally wear down their nails, although many will still need an occasional nail trim. Depending on how your pet reacts to trimming, it may be done at home by you, by a groomer, or by a veterinary technician in your veterinarian's office.

If you do trim your pet's nails at home, go slow and be gentle, as some animals are very sensitive to having their feet handled for a number of reasons. After receiving instruction on how to do this, stay well away from the quick—the pink part of the nail that is visible unless your pet has dark or black nails. The quick contains nerves and a blood supply. If you do accidently cut the quick, you will know this as your pet will react due to pain, and it will bleed. See Chapter 16 for what to do if you trim your pet's nails too short.

When looking at your pet's nails, pay attention to:

- The length of all nails, including dewclaws and the extra toes that some animals have. Some nails are hidden and easily forgotten about but, when overgrown and growing into the pad, can be the source of much pain. Take action to keep nails trimmed and well away from growing into the pad. If you are not comfortable doing this, ask for assistance or request a lesson on how to do this. Going slow at first and only doing a few nails at a time is a good way to get both you and your pet used to this procedure.

- The base of the nails. Is infection, dirt, or fungus present? Is there a bad smell? Healthy feet should not smell bad! Consult with your vet if any of the above is present.

- The pads of the feet. Are they dry and cracked or red and painful? Animals with very furry feet that stay constantly damp from going outside in wet weather or from constant licking are more at risk for infections. Sometimes simply keeping the hair trimmed and the feet dry will help alleviate

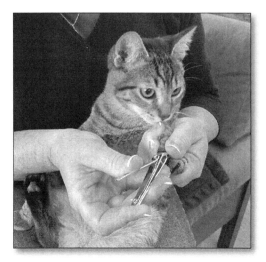

problems. If you live in a snowy area, make sure your dog's feet are free from ice that can collect between the pads when out walking.

Many cats will tolerate a nail trim when held in your lap and facing away from you. You may have to work up to doing all four paws at once. Extra restraint may be needed with this technique if your cat is prone to bite. In this case a cat muzzle would work nicely. (See Chapter 10 for information on muzzles.) Use praise and treats so that your cat does not fear nail trim time.

Bathing Your Pet

A therapeutic bath can provide relief to a pet with a skin condition, and a good, cleaning bath can remove excess oil, dirt, urine, and feces from an animal that has become soiled. Always follow instructions and rinse well after shampooing. Failing to rinse well can cause skin irritation and matting of the fur.

If you think that your pet would benefit from a bath, here are some guidelines:

- Make sure you have all your supplies handy.

- To make sure your pet is comfortable with the process, you may have to introduce it slowly to the idea of getting wet.

- Make sure you use an appropriate shampoo. Read the directions, and *never use a flea shampoo formulated specifically for dogs on a cat, kitten, or even a puppy.* A gentle cleaning shampoo or diluted baby shampoo works well.

- Make sure your pet is on a nonskid surface.

- Make sure you are bathing your pet in a very warm area.

⚘ Make sure your pet has a warm area to be in after bathing. This is especially important for elderly pets. Some people use a blow-dryer after a bath, but be very careful not to overheat your pet.

⚘ Try to remove all mats before bathing, as the water will make the mats tighter and harder to remove or comb out.

Pets with allergies can benefit from being bathed at least twice a month. Normal bathing can also be done that often.

Even in dry weather, it is recommended that allergic dogs have their feet wiped with a damp cloth. This will wipe off any pollen or mold spores that may be present. Tepid or cool water rinses (no shampoo) can be done daily if needed.

Topical flea control products (Frontline/Advantage) should be applied at least two days after a bath or else they may not be effective.

Bathing Cats and Kittens

Bathing cats can be challenging, but here are some helpful tips:

⚘ Trim your cat's or kitten's nails before the bath.

⚘ Remove everything from around the sink. A cat that badly wants to get off the sink will grab at everything it possibly can! You can tie a towel to the faucet to give the cat or kitten something to cling to as you are bathing it.

⚘ Have all your supplies readily at hand. You will need two thick towels, a plastic cup for rinsing, and an appropriate shampoo. You might also want to have combs or brushes to use after the bath. If your cat has mats or tangles and will allow you, comb them out before shampooing them.

⚘ Putting a wiggly cat in a harness can make it easier to hang on to and keep in the bathwater!

A preferred method of bathing cats is as follows:

1. After doing the first two steps above, fill the sink one-third full with warm, soapy water. The soap you use should be pet-appropriate shampoo.

2. Putting cotton balls in the ears can keep water from getting in and dull the sound of the running water that some cats really object to. Just don't forget to remove the cotton balls! Leaving damp cotton balls in the ears can cause infection if they are left there for any length of time.

3. Gently lower the cat into the sink. Using your hand or the plastic cup, gently and slowly pour the warm water over the cat from the shoulders down. Do not pour water on the cat's head! When the cat is wet all over, use a little more shampoo and make sure the cat is nice and sudsy. Don't forget the feet and under the tail. Some shampoos need "contact time," which means you will need to try to keep the shampoo on for a specified amount of time in order for it to be therapeutic. Do the best you can!

4. When you are ready to rinse, let the water out of the sink slowly and gently rinse the cat using a plastic cup, faucet, or handheld sprayer. Always test the water temperature again before rinsing the cat!

5. Rub the cat vigorously with thick, dry towels. Many cats like to be wrapped in another warm, dry towel after this step.

6. Some long-haired cats will allow you to comb their fur out after you have dried them off, but most just will want to get away from you. Don't worry, the cat's tongue will do a good job of rearranging its fur!

7. Place the cat in a very warm environment to dry off or, if it allows, dry it with a blow-dryer.

Some people like to use an ophthalmic lubricating ointment before bathing in case they get shampoo in the animal's eyes. I do not use this method as some animals, especially cats, do not like it and will fight to rub their eyes after it is applied. Just be very careful not to get soapy water in the areas of their eyes.

This bathing method can also be used for small dogs.

Bathing Dogs

Most dogs will reasonably tolerate a bath. If a dog is very large, heavily matted, or very uncooperative, you may want to enlist the services of a groomer or your veterinary team.

1. Choose an area to bathe your dog. It may be a bathtub, large laundry tub, child's pool, or under the garden hose (in warm weather only). Many communities have convenient self-serve dog-wash businesses. Whatever you choose, provide a rubber mat or a nonskid surface for your pet to stand on. This will not only help prevent injury but will also help a dog feel less nervous than if it cannot gain its footing.

2. Unless you don't mind getting wet, wear something waterproof such as a smock or rain jacket.

3. Use an appropriate shampoo. Do not use human shampoo, as it may be drying and irritating to your dog's skin. Do not use flea shampoo on puppies without reading the directions to make sure it is labeled as safe. When possible, do not use over-the-counter flea shampoos.

4. Give your pet a chance to relieve itself before you start. You may also choose to bathe your dog after a nice walk has tired it out!

5. Try to comb out any large mats or tangles.

6. You may want to put cotton balls in your dog's ears. *Remember to remove them after you are done bathing the dog!*

7. Test the water temperature before wetting your pet, and make sure it is comfortably warm. Gently run the water over the dog's shoulders and back to help it get used to the water even if it is not its first bath. Then gradually spray the water toward the head and tail. Apply the shampoo, and lather up the fur. Some therapeutic shampoos achieve their maximum benefit by the "contact time" they require staying on the pet's fur. Check with your veterinarian regarding this. Don't forget to lather up the feet and under the tail.

8. Rinse, rinse, rinse! Then rinse some more. If you don't mind, allow your dog to shake the excess water off. Rub vigorously with thick towels, and allow the dog to dry, or if your pet allows, you can speed up the process using warm air from a blow-dryer.

Waterless or Dry Shampoos

Also available for use on pets are waterless or dry shampoos. These come in a variety of scents and are generally pleasant-smelling foam. These are best used in a pinch for pets that cannot be bathed without risk, such as the geriatric pet that has soiled itself and cannot stand safely in the tub. They are not meant to be a replacement for regular bathing or a cleansing bath, as they really just rinse the hair and do not clean the skin.

Fleas, Ticks, Lice, Maggots, and Other Nasty Critters

Part of keeping your pet's skin and coat healthy is keeping it free of external parasites such as fleas, ticks, lice, and maggots. Not only can these little vermin make your pet uncomfortable, but they can also cause disease, illness, and allergic reactions.

Fleas can infest and make an animal's life miserable even if you do not see them. Using a flea comb, comb your pet thoroughly from behind the ears to the base of the tail. If you see what looks like salt (flea eggs) and pepper (flea "dirt"), your pet has fleas. These can also be seen on a pet's bedding. It can be useful to lay down a white sheet or towel over your pet's bed or where it likes to sleep so you can easily see the evidence of fleas. To differentiate flea dirt from other specks of dirt, tap the dirt on a damp paper towel or in the sink. Flea dirt is actually digested blood from your pet and will look like tiny droplets of blood when wet.

Many pets are allergic to fleas and fleabites and will develop tiny scabs, often around the neck and base of the tail. Chewing at and licking these areas will cause more skin irritation and possibly infection. Fleas can also carry and cause the disease *hemobartonella*. Fleas can also cause anemia, especially in young, elderly, and other immuno-compromised animals.

There are many options for treating fleas. *Never use over-the-counter flea products for cats, even when labeled safe for cats.* Many cats have become seriously ill and have died after the application of an over-the-counter product labeled safe for their use. *Never use a flea product labeled for dogs on your cat.* Some flea products for dogs are so toxic to cats that they can die after exposure to a pet that has recently been treated. Even "all-natural" products have the potential to cause adverse reactions. Your best bet is getting advice from your veterinarian about safe products to use on your pet and in your home to get rid of fleas.

Lice

Lice usually infest very young or elderly animals. Lice are "species specific," so do not worry—you cannot get lice from or give lice to an animal. Infestations of lice are usually not serious and can be treated with a basic topical antiparasitic agent such a flea shampoo. *Again, be careful and do not use over-the-counter flea products, especially on a weak or debilitated pet.* Fipronil, the active ingredient in Frontline or similar generics, is effective at killing lice. Other pets of the same species in contact with the infected pet will also need to be treated. The pet's bedding should be washed in hot, soapy water. Because lice tend to target sick or debilitated animals, if your pet has lice, it is a good idea for it to be examined by your veterinarian for other problems.

Ticks

Ticks are nasty little creatures that can often cause diseases such as Lyme disease, Rocky Mountain spotted fever, and *bartonellosis*, among others. Many of these diseases can also affect people. Ticks bury their heads in the skin and suck the blood of the host animal, usually around the head, neck, ears, and feet. They tend to be most active in the late spring and summer.

Ticks react differently with cats and dogs. There is debate about whether cats can get Lyme disease, but many veterinarians believe that they can become infected with it. Check with your veterinarian for more information about what ticks and tick-borne diseases are found in your area. More information can also be found at www.capcvet.org.

Often, cats and dogs will pick up ticks while walking in the woods and tall grass. Checking your pet daily is important if you live in areas where ticks and tick-borne diseases are present.

Signs of tick-borne illness include lack of appetite, fever, joint pain, and lethargy.

The best way to remove a tick is:

1. Clean a pair of fine-tipped tweezers with rubbing alcohol.

2. Gently cleanse the area where the tick is embedded with rubbing alcohol.

3. If possible, wear rubber gloves.

4. Grasp the tick firmly as close to the skin as possible and pull straight up. Do not squeeze or crush the tick.

5. If the mouthpart of the tick remains in the skin, try to gently remove it. If you are not able to, do not persist as this may cause additional irritation. Seek veterinary advice.

6. Place the tick in a jar with alcohol to kill it.

7. Wash your hands.

8. Monitor the site of the tick removal. It may be itchy to your pet, so make sure it is not licking or biting at the area.

9. Monitor your pet for any possible reactions to the tick bite. Seek veterinary advice at the first sign of illness.

It is important to remember to tell your veterinarian if your pet has traveled to other parts of the country should it become ill with an unknown illness.

Maggots

Now here's a subject nobody likes to think about, but maggots can be a very unfortunate consequence of leaving an elderly or compromised animal outside in warm weather. Flies will look for a warm, damp, and dark place to lay eggs. Open wounds and the soft tissue under an animal's tail are prime targets for flies to lay eggs. In addition, flies will also seek out any bit of feces on a sedentary pet's hair coat and lay eggs. The eggs hatch and turn into larvae, also called maggots.

Emergency treatment of maggots is usually necessary. Use extreme caution when leaving animals that may be susceptible to maggots outside for any length of time. While it is wonderful to get them outside for fresh air, they must be monitored.

Ringworm

Ringworm is not actually a worm but is caused by a fungus. There are three different fungi that can cause ringworm, but *Microsporum canis* is the most common. The fungus infects the superficial layers of the skin and causes, to varying degrees, redness, itching, and hair loss. This is a zoonotic disease, meaning that it is a disease that people can also get.

Ringworm gets its name by the characteristic ring that forms on the skin. The fungus causes circular areas of red skin accompanied by hair loss. It is often found on the ears, face, and feet. Animals get this fungus from infected soil or another infected animal.

Ringworm is diagnosed by plucking a few hairs and attempting to culture the fungus on a special growing medium. The results can take up to three weeks to culture. *Microsporum canis* grows fairly pretty quickly, but *Trichophyton*, another fungus that can cause ringworm, can take two to three weeks. A blacklight can also be used to illuminate the fungus on an animal's skin in a dark room. This method is not foolproof, as other things (dust, powder, lint, etc.) may also fluoresce.

Ringworm can be self-limiting, although it can also be difficult to clear on an immune-compromised animal, such as young or elderly animals. Self limiting means it will generally run its course and clear up without treatment. Sunlight and keeping a clean environment can help to clear infections, although veterinary care and prescription medications are also often needed to clear up cases of ringworm.

Reinfection tends to be the main reason ringworm is hard to treat. Environmental decontamination is very important. As

Dr. Ashley says: "Adopt this principle: Think like a cat hair. Wherever it can and will go (and they go everywhere), you need to clean that spot."

As always, ask your veterinarian for advice on any skin issues that may arise. Your pet will greatly appreciate your efforts to keep it clean, comfortable, and free of infection, parasites, and any other unwanted "friends"!

⚬❦⚬

CHAPTER 12

The Feline Birthing Process

What you will learn in this chapter:

- ❧ What the estrus, or "heat," cycles are

- ❧ What the gestation period for cats is

- ❧ What behavior to expect from pregnant cats

- ❧ What to expect as delivery time approaches

- ❧ What the signs of labor are

- ❧ What the delivery process is

- ❧ How to recognize problems in the delivery process

- ❧ When and how to help the mother cat

- ❧ What care is needed after the kittens are born

- ❧ A sweet story

Homeless cats and kittens are a problem in most communities. Even if you have homes in mind for them, it is far kinder not to breed your cat. If you have a strong desire to witness the birthing process and watch the development of kittens, humane societies and rescue organizations are always looking for foster homes for late-term pregnant cats and orphaned kittens.

A Cat in "Heat"

An unspayed cat is called a queen. A female cat, or queen, comes into "heat" (estrus) several times each year. A cat has four stages in her estrous cycle (proestrus, estrus, diestrus, and anestrus) and a nonestrous interval between cycles. Cats do not bleed during the proestrus cycles like dogs, so the physical signs may not be as noticeable as in a dog.

Estrus is defined as a period of breeding in unspayed dogs, cats, and other animals. The period that a female cat will be fertile and have receptive behavior lasts for six to seven days on average, but it can also last from one to twenty-one days. If not bred during a heat cycle, a female cat will enter a nonestrous period, which may last two to nineteen days (average eight days) before starting a heat cycle again.

The number of daylight hours is a major factor in the timing of when the heat cycles start. Indoor-only cats may have irregular heat cycles due to exposure to both artificial and natural light. Temperature can have a lesser influence on the start of a heat cycle. Most cats in a temperate climate will start heat cycles in January or February, with the most activity seen in February and March.

Estrous can occur in cats as young as five months old, although six to twelve months old is more common. A cat can get pregnant as young as five or six months old, when she is still a kitten herself. The most noticeable sign of the estrus period is the change in her behavior. The cat may become very adamant in getting her demands met or become very affectionate, often rubbing up against her owners and sometimes objects. A cat in heat often becomes very vocal—at all hours—and rolls on the floor. When petted along its back, it may lift its hind end, turn its tail to the side or straight up like a tomcat spraying, and tread with its back legs. Occasionally, it may fall to the floor. Sometimes this behavior is so unusual that people fear their cats may be having seizures or be in pain. One thing is certain—even the most devoted cat lover will have a hard time tolerating this behavior.

Often, people will put the cat outside, not realizing what is going on and then be surprised a few weeks later when the cat starts to gain weight. Another unwanted result is that cats in heat will attract intact (not neutered) male cats. These tomcats will appear and often try to get to the cat in heat. If necessary, tomcats will travel a great distance to find a female in heat and are often the carriers of feline immunodeficiency virus (FIV).

In addition to the behavioral changes and risk of pregnancy, there is also a risk of infections. Feline leukemia virus (FeLV) and FIV are spread between cats through saliva and blood. Since females in heat will attract multiple male cats, cats are at higher risk for becoming infected both due to fights and in the mating process if they come into contact with infected cats. These diseases may then be transmitted to the unborn kittens.

Cats are induced ovulators, which mean that they only release eggs from their ovaries when they are mated. Therefore, the queen can become pregnant at any time while she is in heat. When she breeds with a tomcat, the barbs on his penis stimulate the inside of the vaginal vault, which induces hormones that make the ovaries release eggs. When this happens, the female's eggs are present in the reproductive tract just as sperm is deposited. Cats will often mate with more than one tomcat and can have a litter of kittens with different fathers. A kitten may be up to one week younger than the rest of the litter. These are often the kittens that are called runts. The length of estrus (breeding phase) is not changed by successful fertilization and will last an average of six to seven days.

The Gestation Period

The period of pregnancy is also called the gestation period. It generally ranges from sixty to sixty-seven days. Pregnancy becomes noticeable around the fourth week. A cat that is getting close to the end of her pregnancy will often look pear-shaped and lumpy on her sides. You may feel kittens moving if you place your hand lightly on her sides. The mammary glands enlarge, and her nipples become more noticeable as the birth of the kittens approaches.

A pregnant cat should be fed very high-quality kitten food for the duration of the pregnancy and throughout the nursing period. You can find these types of foods at pet health food stores, veterinary hospitals, or pet supply stores. Being high in protein and vital nutrients, kitten diets provide all the extra nutrition needed for the nursing mother and her kittens. Nursing cats that are eating one of these diets need no other supplements. She should be encouraged to eat as much as she likes during this time and may consume about 50 percent more than before pregnancy. She needs to eat this much to meet her own nutritional needs and those of the kittens.

Behavior of Pregnant Cats

A pregnant cat may show some behavioral changes. Many become very loving toward humans and may require more affection and attention. Some cats may act the opposite way and become intolerant and cranky. Keep in mind that most mother cats are excellent mothers, some to the point of becoming aggressive with other animals or becoming intolerant of anyone she perceives as a threat. It is very important that she feels safe and comfortable as the time comes for the birth of her kittens.

As the pregnancy progresses, some cats become uncomfortable being left alone and will want to stay close to their person or family.

Cats rarely get morning sickness, but some may vomit a little more than normal at the beginning of their pregnancies.

As the Delivery Time Approaches

As the time of labor becomes closer, many cats try to find a place to make their "nest," or birthing place. Well in advance of the time of delivery, a queening or birthing box should be placed in a quiet place away from household activity. A closet or a small area in a quiet room may work well, although often what people think is an appropriate place may not be to the cat's liking. Show her several different places, and let her choose. The box itself should be large enough for the cat to move and turn around in. The box should be half again as long as the cat. It should have one low side. This will make it easier for her to get in and out as well as to allow her to see out. The box should be lined with several layers of white paper towels or other disposable, absorbent material. Newspaper should not be used, as the ink can be toxic to the cat and kittens when it gets wet. Underpads for human use or puppy training pads work very well. These will absorb any fluid that comes from the birthing process. Using multiple layers makes it easier to remove a soiled layer with minimal disruption to the mother and her newborn kittens.

Signs of Labor

Some of the signs of impending labor are:

- Restless behavior that may include nervousness and pacing

- Vocalizing

- Mammary glands that are suddenly engorged with milk

- Refusal to eat for about twenty-four hours

- A drop in rectal temperature, to less than 100°F (37.8°C). The cat's temperature may drop intermittently for several days prior to delivery but will remain low for the twenty-four hours prior to delivery.

Labor and Delivery

Most cats do not have problems when delivering kittens. Some cats, however, are tiny themselves or are very young when they give birth to their own kittens. These cats and any first-time mothers should be watched during the entire labor process. If the first two kittens are born quickly and easily and the mother seems to know what to do, you can monitor her from a distance. However, young or thin cats may become tired and should be monitored closely for difficulty delivering the last kittens. Occasionally a cat will want to follow her caretaker as he or she leaves the room, even while giving birth. Sitting down next to her while she is in her queening box may make her feel more at ease.

The Delivery Process

The act of giving birth is called parturition. The time it takes for cats to give birth may vary. It is thought that cats having slim heads, such as Siamese, Oriental Shorthairs, etc., may deliver quicker, often in one to two hours. Cats having large, round heads may take longer to deliver their kittens.

Kittens are most often born head first, with the nose/muzzle and tops of the front feet showing. They may also present with the bottoms of the hind feet and tail showing. It is unusual for kittens to be born breech, meaning the kitten is delivered with its tail showing (but with no feet showing). This is abnormal, and veterinary care should be sought at once.

Each kitten is enclosed in its own sac. The sac is part of the placenta. The placenta is also called the afterbirth. It is normal for the mother to eat the placenta. The placenta may be delivered as the kitten is being born or shortly after.

The average time of parturition is about three to six hours.

What you will see as delivery begins:

- The mother cat will lie down, and her breathing will begin to get quicker. She may breathe with her mouth open. She may make soft grunts or noises.

- Contractions may look like ripples along her lower body as she tries to bear down and discharge the kitten.

- A fluid-filled sac will appear in the mother's vagina after passing through the birth canal.

In a normal delivery, first-stage contractions will come about every ten to fifteen minutes and last about fifteen to thirty seconds. The contractions will increase in strength and duration. A few strong contractions should discharge the kitten. Next, the mother will tear open the sac and use her tongue to lick the kitten's nose and mouth to clear it of fluids. She will then vigorously lick its body. While this may look rough and you may worry she is going to injure the kitten, this vigorous washing is needed to stimulate circulation. This also causes the kitten to cry and begin breathing. Additionally, it cleans and dries the kitten's fur.

Young and inexperienced mothers may not know what to do, and without your intervention, the kitten will suffocate. (See When and How to Help below.) The mother will then chew on and sever the umbilical cord about three-fourths to one inch from the body. Lastly, she will eat the placenta. In larger litters, it is best to only let the mother eat two to three placentas, as ingesting more may cause vomiting or diarrhea, or both.

The time between kittens being delivered may be irregular, and the mother may rest up to an hour between kittens being born.

Dystocia—Trouble Giving Birth

The term *dystocia* means slow or difficult labor or delivery. Dystocia may require surgical intervention. The general health condition and size of the mother, the size of the litter, and the size of the kittens are some of the determining factors. Ideally, an X-ray should be taken before labor starts to determine the number of kittens and their size relative to the mother. This is extremely useful in order to know when all kittens have been born.

Seek veterinary care if any of the following occur:

- Intense labor contractions for more than forty-five minutes without a kitten being born.

- A period of longer than two hours between kittens, with no contractions. Knowing how many kittens are present will help determine if the mother cat is done or is having trouble.

- Intense labor of more than twenty minutes when a kitten is visible in the birth canal. This will look like a fluid-filled sac.

- The sac appears with contractions then retracts back into the birth canal.

- The mother becomes suddenly lethargic or exhausted.

- Contractions cease and no kitten has been born.

- The mother's body temperature is higher than 103°F (39.4°C) when taken with a rectal thermometer.

- The mother's mucus membranes (gum color) become whitish or bluish. Seek immediate veterinary care if you see this. These signs may signal a life-threatening condition.

- There is a large amount of fresh bloody discharge from the birth canal for more than ten minutes.

- There is any amount of foul-smelling liquid or discharge coming from the birth canal.

- Parturition that goes on longer than six hours.

- The mother shows signs of weakness and is unable to stand after giving birth.

When and How to Help

First, wash your hands with soap and hot water! You do not want to introduce bacteria to a newborn kitten.

If after ten minutes of the sac being visible in the birth canal but no kitten emerges:

- Using a damp square of gauze or a clean, thin washcloth, break the sac and very gently grasp the head or feet. When the next contraction occurs, apply firm but gentle traction in the direction of the mother's tail using a downward curved forty-five-degree arc. If the kitten does not move easily or the mother cries out, seek immediate veterinary care. Do not pull with force, as you can easily break a bone or the kitten's neck or tear the mother's birth canal.

If the mother does not remove the sac within one minute after delivery:

- Using a damp square of gauze or a thin washcloth, break the sac, wipe the kitten's face, and pull away the sac. Do not separate the kitten from the sac until the umbilical cord is tied off and cut. Rub the kitten's body gently but vigorously with a soft, warm towel to stimulate circulation and dry the hair.

- Make sure the kitten stays warm by using either warmed towels or a heating pad while the kitten is being dried.

- Tie the umbilical cord with sewing thread or dental floss about a half inch (1.3 cm) from the body. Tie another piece about a quarter inch (0.6 cm) between the first tie and the sac.

- Cut the umbilical cord between the two tied pieces of thread or floss using scissors that have been cleaned with alcohol and allowed to dry.

If you hear a rasping sound coming from the kitten or the kitten's tongue appears bluish:

Newborn kittens may have fluid in their lungs, which is why you may hear raspy sounds when they breathe. In addition, a bluish tongue indicates they are not getting sufficient oxygen into their lungs. When an animal is getting adequate oxygen, its tongue will appear pink or red.

- Using a pediatric (infant) ear syringe, gently suction any fluid out of the kitten's nose and mouth. Do not swing the kitten downward, as this forces the surfactant, or normal lung fluid needed for the lungs to open, out of the lungs and also forces fluid from the stomach, increasing the risk of choking or aspirating.

- Use acupuncture on GV 26 (Governing Vessel 26) to stimulate breathing. See Chapter 16 for detailed information.

Try to leave the kittens with the mother to nurse. It is important for kittens to start nursing within the first two hours of life. Also, nursing stimulates uterine contractions and can help with labor.

If the mother cat is in distress and requires assistance, or if she is being aggressive toward the kittens, you may need to separate the newborn kittens as she continues to give birth. Have available a small, clean, dry box lined with fluffy, warm material such as towels or fake lambswool for the newborn kittens. A towel can be warmed in a microwave oven for less than thirty seconds or thrown in the dryer on high heat for a few minutes. Use extreme caution if microwaving to avoid burning. A stable kitten with a tied cord can be placed in this box while the mother is continuing to deliver the rest of her litter. Keeping the kittens warm is vital to their survival, and supplemental heat must be supplied. Even warm room air is not warm enough. You may use a heating pad with a heating element made specifically for pets, a hot-water bottle, or a SnuggleSafe heating disc and place it in the box. Use great caution when using any of these, including a heat lamp. If using a heating pad, place it on the lowest setting. *Make sure that any heat source in the bottom of the box is covered with layers of material so that there is no danger of burning the kittens.* Newborn kittens may be unable to move away from the heat source. Also, never leave a heat lamp unattended or place it closer than five feet from the box.

Care After Delivery

Once the mother cat has finished delivering her kittens, any soiled material should be removed from the queening box. Do this with a minimum of disturbance to the mother and her new family. If a mother cat seems very stressed by your intrusion, try again in a few hours. You do not want the mother cat to feel threatened and to move her kittens. The mother should now accept the kittens readily and be resting comfortably on her side to allow the kittens to nurse.

Whenever possible, have the mother and her litter examined by a veterinarian within twenty-four hours after the delivery is completed. This will help to ensure there are no undelivered kittens and to check the health of the mother and the newborn kittens. It is also a great time to ask your veterinarian any questions you have regarding behavior and nutrition and to discuss when to have the mother safely spayed. Most communities have veterinarians who will come to your home for this service so you do not have to move the whole kit and kaboodle.

The mother cat will often be very tired and will want to rest even while the kittens are nursing or sleeping. Although she will be tired, she should also be fairly bright, alert, and attentive to her babies. She may also be very hungry. Resist the temptation to reward her efforts with a large meal; she needs to be fed several small meals a day rather than one large one. Place the food a short distance from the birthing box, as the mother may be reluctant to leave her kittens. Always have plenty of fresh water available for her close by. It is also a good idea to have a clean litter box a short distance away. It is very important that the litter box be cleaned continuously. She may not be comfortable having a dirty litter box near her kittens and may move them as a result.

A mother's mammary glands should be checked to make sure they are producing milk. If the kittens are restless and fussy, they may be hungry. See Chapter 14 for information on bottle-feeding babies that are not getting enough milk. It is best to keep them with the mother even if you are bottle-feeding them.

Check the mother's mammary glands daily for signs of a painful breast infection called mastitis. Usually only one or two teats are affected at a time. Signs of mastitis include heat, red or black coloration, mammary glands that are firm or hard to the touch, and pain. Other signs are milk that is thick or lumpy and has a pink, red, green, or yellow tinge. Do not confuse this with the colostrum, the milk produced in the first twenty-four to forty-eight hours, which normally has a yellow color. Do not allow the kittens to nurse from the infected teats, and seek veterinary care immediately. To prevent them from nursing, you can put a baby's T-shirt on the mother or use a piece of stockinette. (Stockinette is a tubular stretchy knit fabric. It can be obtained from your veterinarian or medical supply store.) The kittens may nurse from any teats that appear normal.

It is normal for the mother to have a bloody vaginal discharge for several days following delivery. This discharge is called the lochia and consists of tissue and fluids from the uterus. Normal lochia color is usually amber to brick-red but can also be greenish-black or brownish. Consult your veterinarian at once if the lochia is bright red or becomes thick, gray, or light colored or has a foul odor. This may indicate a retained placenta or a uterine infection. By the second week, the lochia should be clear mucus.

Also be on the alert for *eclampsia,* also called "milk fever." This is a calcium deficiency that occurs in nursing mothers. Signs of eclampsia include excessive restlessness, difficulty walking, panting, muscle tremors, elevated temperature, and vocalizing. If you see any of these signs, seek veterinary care immediately. Left untreated, this can lead to limb rigidity, seizures, collapse, and eventual death. Treatment can be very successful when eclampsia is caught early.

Seek veterinary care if at any time the mother shows signs of fever, lack of appetite, depression, or reluctance to care for her young.

If the mother leaves the box unattended for any length of time, it is important to provide heat for the kittens as described above and in Chapter 14.

Premature Kittens

It is not common for kittens to be born prematurely, although they may be born early as the result of infection or trauma. These kittens may be very fragile—small, thin, and often with little or no hair. Mortality is extremely high for premature kittens. To determine if the kitten is full-term, look at the tops of the paws. If there is hair present, they are full-term or close to full-term. Kittens weighing less than three ounces at birth also have a high mortality rate and should be monitored hourly to encourage eating. Often, with premature kittens, the mother's milk is not yet being produced. If the mother has milk available, it is important to encourage the kittens to nurse naturally. If the mother has no milk available, care for them as you would orphaned kittens. Please see Chapter 14 for detailed information on caring for orphaned kittens.

A Sweet Story

Several days before Mother's Day in 2011, I got a call from an acquaintance who had been feeding a stray cat. Because he was allergic to cats, he had made her a little shelter outside and fed her well. He called to tell me he thought she had gained a lot of weight since she first showed up. He was wondering if her weight gain was because she was pregnant and if I could come take a look at her. I went right over and found a sweet cat that was so far along in pregnancy that I thought she might start to give birth as we stood there. I took her home with me and quickly set her up in a warm, quiet place with a birthing box. She got right into the box and settled in, and I went to prepare a meal for her. When I came back, she was in the early stages of labor. Having only known her for about half an hour, I wasn't sure how she would feel about me being so close, but she reached out her paw, put it down on my hand, and softly meowed. I promised her I would stay, and shortly after that, the first of her eight kittens was born! Isis, as I immediately named her, was a wonderful and devoted mother. She and her eight kittens all got spayed and neutered and found fantastic forever homes. I think of them every year on Mother's Day!

CHAPTER 13

The Canine Birthing Process

What you will learn in this chapter:

ᴗ What the estrus, or "heat," cycles are

ᴗ What the gestation period for dogs is

ᴗ What behavior to expect from pregnant dogs

ᴗ What to expect as delivery time approaches

ᴗ What the signs of labor are

ᴗ What the delivery process is

ᴗ How to recognize problems in the delivery process

ᴗ When and how to help the mother dog

ᴗ What care is needed after the puppies are born

Although there are usually not as many stray dogs and puppies as cats and kittens roaming the streets in most areas, that is no reason to randomly breed puppies—even if they are adorable. And as with kittens, even if you have homes in mind for the resulting puppies, it is far kinder to not breed your dog. If you have a strong desire to witness the birthing process and watch the development of puppies, humane societies and rescue organizations are always looking for foster homes for late-term pregnant dogs and orphaned puppies.

A Dog in "Heat"

A female dog (bitch) comes into "heat" (estrus) several times each year. Estrus is defined as a period of sexual receptivity in unspayed dogs, cats, and other animals. During this time, the dog's estrogen levels will increase and then decrease, followed by mature eggs being released from the ovaries. An unspayed dog's first estrus usually occurs when she is about six to twenty-four months old. It tends to occur earlier in small-breed dogs than in large-breed dogs.

Depending on breed and the individual dog, this period lasts for approximately fifteen to twenty days and, if she is not bred, repeats about twice a year. Although males may be attracted to her for this entire period, she may only be receptive to them for breeding about half the time.

Behavioral changes are evident during a dog's estrus period. She may act anxious or skittish, and she may also urinate more often than normal. These signs are due to hormonal changes in her body. In the presence of male dogs, she may signal her receptivity by tensing and elevating her hind end and holding her tail to one side. Because both intact males and females will go to great lengths, literally traveling miles, to find each other during estrus, it is very important that your dog not be allowed to escape or wander. Many dogs become lost or are hit by cars in the pursuit of finding a mate.

Physically, you may notice the female has a blood-tinged vaginal discharge and her vulva is swollen. The discharge will lessen in amount and change from blood-tinged to straw-colored when she is receptive to male dogs.

The Gestation Period

The period of pregnancy is called the gestation period. It generally ranges from sixty to sixty-eight days. Pregnancy becomes noticeable around the fourth week. A dog that is getting close to the end of her pregnancy will often look lumpy on her sides.

A pregnant dog should be fed a very high-quality food that is labeled for dogs and puppies for the duration of the pregnancy and throughout the nursing period. You can find these types of foods at pet health food stores, veterinary hospitals, and pet supply stores. Being high in protein and vital nutrients, puppy diets provide all the extra nutrition needed for the nursing mother and her puppies. When nursing dogs are eating one of these diets, no other supplements are needed. The mother dog should be encouraged to eat as much as she likes during this time as she may consume over 50 percent more than before pregnancy. She needs to eat this much to meet her own nutritional needs and those of her growing puppies.

Behavior of Pregnant Dogs

A pregnant dog may show some behavioral changes. As with cats, many become very loving toward humans and may require more affection and attention. Some act quite the opposite and become intolerant and cranky. Most dogs are excellent mothers, some to the point of becoming aggressive with other animals or becoming intolerant of anyone they perceive as a threat. It is very important that the mother dog feels safe and comfortable as the time comes for the birth of her puppies. Some dogs become uncomfortable being left alone and will want to stay close to their person or family.

Dogs rarely experience morning sickness, but some may vomit a little more than normal at the beginning of their pregnancies or as labor begins. Persistent vomiting is abnormal.

As the Delivery Time Approaches

As the time of labor becomes closer, many dogs will try to find a place to make their birthing, or whelping, place. Well in advance of the time of delivery, a whelping box should be placed in a quiet place away from household activity. A closet or a small area in a quiet room may work well, although often what people think is an appropriate place is not to the dog's liking. Show her several different places, and let her choose. The box itself should be large enough for her to move and turn around in. It should have one low side. This will make it easier for the mother dog to get in and out as well as to see out. Many people with large dogs will use a child's swimming pool for the whelping box. The box should be lined with several layers of white paper towels or other disposable, absorbent material. Newspaper can be used, although the ink can get on the mother and puppies when it gets wet. There is some concern about toxicity from the ink, so use newspaper only if nothing else is available. Underpads for human use and puppy training pads work very well. These will absorb any fluid that comes from the birthing process. Using multiple layers makes it easier to remove a soiled layer with minimal disruption to the mother and her newborn puppies.

Signs of Labor

Some of the signs of impending labor are:

- Restless behavior that may include nervousness and pacing

- Searching for a place to make a nest or scratching at the floor

- Whining or other vocalizing

- Mammary glands that are suddenly engorged with milk

- Refusal to eat for about twenty-four hours before labor

- A drop in rectal temperature, to less than 100°F (37.8°C). The mother's temperature may drop intermittently for several days prior to delivery, but it will remain low for twenty-four hours prior to delivery.

Labor and Delivery

Most dogs do not have problems with delivering puppies. Some large dogs, such as labs, give birth to small puppies, whereas some terriers have smaller litters with larger puppies. Some dogs are tiny themselves or are very young and inexperienced when they give birth to their own puppies. Some breeds of dogs, such as bulldogs and other large-headed dogs, may be more likely to have difficulty giving birth. It is very important to line up emergency veterinary care for them well in advance. These dogs and any first-time mothers should be watched carefully.

A dog may want to follow her caretaker as he or she leaves the room, even while giving birth. Sitting down next to the mother dog while she is in her whelping box may make her feel more at ease.

The Delivery Process

In advance of labor starting, assemble the supplies that you may possibly need. Have readily available a stack of clean, soft towels, thread or dental floss for tying off umbilical cords, hand disinfectant if you do not have access to soap and water, and a disinfected pair of scissors. Once labor begins, you may want to be in phone contact with your veterinarian to let him or her know the birth is starting and in anticipation of any possible problems.

What you will see as delivery begins:

- The mother dog may circle in her bed and try several times to get comfortable. She will then lie down, and her breathing will begin to get quicker.

- She may breathe with her mouth open. She may whine or softly grunt.

- Contractions will begin as she tries to bear down and discharge the puppies.

✧ A fluid-filled sac will appear in her vagina, which is also called the birth canal.

The first stage of labor is when the contractions begin, the cervix begins to soften and open, and the birth canal dilates. These signs may not be very noticeable. The second stage of labor is when the contractions increase in intensity, frequency, and duration. The first puppy should be born within thirty minutes of intense contractions.

In a normal delivery, a few strong contractions will discharge the puppy, usually within ten minutes. Next, the mother will tear open the sac and use her tongue to lick the puppy's nose and mouth to clear it of fluids. She will then vigorously lick its body. While this may look rough and you may worry she is going to injure the puppy, this vigorous washing is needed to stimulate circulation. This is also causes the puppy to cry and begin breathing. Additionally, it cleans and dries the puppy's fur.

Each puppy is enclosed in its own sac. The sac is part of the placenta. The placenta is also called the afterbirth. It is normal for the mother to eat the placenta. The placenta may be delivered as the puppy is being born or shortly after.

Young and inexperienced mothers may not know what to do, and without your intervention, the puppy will suffocate. (See When and How to Help below.) The mother will then chew on and sever the umbilical cord about three-fourths to one inch from the body. Lastly, she will eat the placenta.

Dystocia—Trouble Giving Birth

The term *dystocia* means slow or difficult labor or delivery. Dystocia may require surgical intervention. Often, the general health condition and size of the mother, the size of the litter, and the size of the puppies are the determining factors.

Seek veterinary care at once if any of the following occur:

- ꙮ Intense contractions for more than thirty minutes without a puppy being born.

- ꙮ Intense contractions for more than ten minutes when a puppy is visible in the birth canal. The puppy will look like a fluid-filled sac or bubble.

- ꙮ The mother's body temperature is higher than 103ºF (39.4ºC) when taken with a rectal thermometer.

- ꙮ There is a large amount of fresh bloody discharge from the birth canal for more than ten minutes.

- ꙮ There is any amount of foul-smelling liquid or discharge coming from the birth canal.

- ꙮ There are few or no contractions for one to two hours after a puppy has been born.

- ꙮ A puppy is stuck in the birth canal and isn't moving.

- ꙮ Two puppies are stuck in the birth canal at the same time.

- ꙮ The mother dog shows signs of pain, is lethargic, shaky, or unable to stand.

When and How to Help

First step, wash your hands with soap and hot water! If you are not able to wash, use plenty of hand sanitizer and wait for your hands to dry. You do not want to introduce bacteria to a newborn puppy.

If after ten minutes of the sac being visible, no puppy emerges:

- Using a damp square of gauze or a clean, thin washcloth, break the sac and *very gently* grasp the head or feet. When the next contraction occurs, apply firm but gentle traction in the direction of the mother's tail. If you are unsuccessful or the mother cries out, seek immediate veterinary care.

If the sac is not removed within a few minutes after delivery:

- Using a damp square of gauze or a thin washcloth, break the sac, wipe the puppy's face, and pull away the placenta. *Do not separate the puppy from the sac until the umbilical cord is tied off and cut.* Rub the puppy's body gently but vigorously with a soft, warm towel to stimulate circulation and dry the hair.

- Tie the umbilical cord with cord (sewing thread or dental floss work well) about a half inch (1.3 cm) from the body. Tie another piece about a quarter inch (0.6 cm) between the first tie and the sac.

- Cut the umbilical cord between the two tied pieces of floss or string using clean scissors.

If you hear a rasping sound coming from the puppy or the puppy's tongue appears bluish:

Newborn puppies may have fluid in their lungs, which is why you may hear raspy sounds when they breathe. In addition, bluish tongues indicate they are not getting sufficient oxygen into their lungs. When any animal is getting adequate oxygen, its tongue will appear pink or red.

- Using a pediatric ear syringe, gently suction any fluid out of the puppy's nose and mouth. The downward swinging procedure many people were taught to remove fluid from newborns is no longer thought to be an appropriate method of removing fluid.

This method may actually force the surfactant, or normal lung fluid needed for the lungs to open, out of the lungs, and it also forces fluid from the stomach, increasing the risk of choking or aspirating.

🦴 See Chapter 16 for how to stimulate breathing using an acupuncture technique GV26 (Governing Vessel 26)..

If you are assisting the mother dog, you may need to separate the newborn puppies as she continues to give birth. Have available a small, clean, dry box lined with fluffy, warm material such as towels or fake lambswool for the newborn puppies. A towel can be warmed in a microwave oven or thrown in the dryer on high heat for a few minutes. (Use extreme caution if microwaving!) A stable puppy with a tied cord can be placed in this box while the mother is continuing to deliver the rest of her litter. Keeping the puppies warm is vital to their survival, and supplemental heat must be supplied. Even warm room air is not warm enough. You may use a heating pad, a heating element made specifically for pets, a hot-water bottle, or a SnuggleSafe heating disc, and place it in the box. Use great caution when using any of these, including a heat lamp. If using a heating pad, place it on the lowest setting. *Make sure that any heat source in the bottom of the box is covered with layers of material so that there is no danger of burning the puppies.* Newborn puppies may be unable to move away from the heat source. Also, do not leave a heat lamp unattended.

Care After Delivery

Once the mother dog has finished delivering her puppies, remove any soiled material from the whelping box. Do this with a minimum of disturbance to the mother and her new family. If she seems very stressed by your intrusion, try again in a few hours. You do not want the mother to feel threatened and to move her puppies. The mother should now accept the puppies readily and be resting comfortably on her side, allowing them to nurse.

The mother dog will often be very tired and may want to sleep even while the puppies are nursing or sleeping. Although she will be tired, she should also be fairly bright, alert, and attentive to her babies. She may also be very hungry. Resist the temptation to reward her efforts with a large meal; she needs to be fed several small meals a day rather than one large one. Along with her regular diet, she may enjoy small servings of cottage cheese, liver, or even scrambled eggs! Place the food a short distance from the whelping box, as the mother may be reluctant to leave her puppies. Always have plenty of fresh water available for her close by. Offer her periodic opportunities to relieve herself close by as well.

Especially for very large or inexperienced mothers, it is important to monitor that they do not accidently lie on or squash a newborn puppy.

Check the mother dog's mammary glands daily for signs of a painful breast infection called mastitis. Signs of mastitis include heat, redness, swelling, inflammation, discoloration, and pain. Other signs are milk that is thick or lumpy and has a pink, red, green, or yellow tinge. Do not allow the puppies to nurse from her, and *seek veterinary care immediately*. Follow instructions in Chapter 14 for bottle-feeding puppies. It is important that the puppies stay with the mother if possible, but they cannot be allowed to nurse. To prevent them from nursing, you can gently tuck a towel around the mother's abdomen so the puppies do not have access to her nipples. A T-shirt can also be used for this purpose.

If possible, have the mother and her litter examined by a veterinarian within twenty-four hours after the delivery is completed. This will help to ensure there are no undelivered puppies, and the veterinarian can check the health of the mother and the newborns. It is also a great time to ask your veterinarian any questions you have regarding behavior and nutrition and to discuss when to safely have the mother spayed. Most communities have veterinarians that will come to your home or farm to perform the examinations.

It is normal for the mother to have a vaginal discharge for up to several weeks following delivery. This discharge is called the lochia and consists of tissue and fluids from the uterus. Normal lochia color can be greenish-black, brownish, or brick-red. Consult your veterinarian at once if the lochia becomes thick, gray, or light-colored or has a foul odor. This may indicate a retained placenta or a uterine infection.

Also be on the alert for eclampsia, also called "milk fever." This is a calcium deficiency that occurs within the first four weeks after delivery. Signs of eclampsia include excessive restlessness, panting, muscle tremors, elevated temperature, and vocalizing. Left untreated, this can lead to limb rigidity, seizures, collapse, and eventual death. Treatment with calcium injections and supplements are very successful when eclampsia is caught early.

Premature Puppies

It is not common for puppies to be born prematurely. A miscalculation in whelping dates is usually the reason people think puppies have come early. Occasionally, they may be born early as the result of stress or trauma. The puppies may be very fragile—small, thin, and often with little or no hair. Care for them as you would orphaned puppies, but if possible, keep them with the mother. Please see Chapter 14 for detailed information on caring for orphaned puppies.

CHAPTER 14
Newborn (Neonatal) Kitten and Puppy Care

What you will learn in this chapter:

- When to use feline and canine foster moms

- Facts about newborn kittens

- Facts about newborn puppies

- What supplies you will need

- How to house newborns

- How to feed newborns

- How to use commercial replacement formulas

- What colostrum is and why it is important

- How to make emergency homemade formulas

- How often and how much to feed kittens

- How often and how much to feed puppies

- How to feed from a nursing bottle

- How to monitor weight

- ❧ **How to bottle-feed a kitten or puppy**

- ❧ **How to tube-feed a kitten or puppy**

- ❧ **What the steps are for tube-feeding a kitten or puppy**

- ❧ **How to stimulate an animal to urinate and defecate**

- ❧ **How to wean kittens and puppies**

- ❧ **What abnormal suckling behavior of kittens and puppies is**

- ❧ **How to tell the sex of kittens and puppies**

- ❧ **What some health concerns of kittens and puppies are**

- ❧ **When to vaccinate kittens and puppies**

Caring for newborn kittens and puppies can be very challenging but extremely rewarding. The time commitment can be very large, but watching their development will be well worth it. Providing for their nutritional and emotional needs from the very start can ensure a healthy and well-socialized pet companion.

You may need to bottle or tube-feed a newborn animal for several reasons. Something may have happened to the mother, she may be malnourished and not producing enough milk, or she may have an infection of the mammary glands. Other possible reasons are that the babies may have gotten separated when the mother was in the process of moving them or they may not be getting their fair share of milk.

Some people will tell you not to name an orphaned animal in case it doesn't survive. But I believe that every kitten or puppy deserves a name. Give the animal a name that has a loving connotation to you. Or name it after a brave and strong person or animal that you admire.

Speak its name quietly, and give it all the positive energy you can. Sound, touch, and loving intention are excellent ways to gently help any animal establish a presence in this world. Let the animal know it is loved all the time, even when you are craving sleep!

Feline and Canine Foster Moms

From a behavioral and nutritional standpoint, it is always best for a newborn animal to be raised by a natural mother. The mother will feed it, help socialize it, and keep it warm and clean. Finding a foster mother for orphan kittens or puppies may be possible through local humane societies, animal shelters, or rescue groups. If you have one or two orphans, they can usually be incorporated into another litter, and some mothers will accept another litter after they are finished nursing their own. This should be used as a temporary situation, as it is very taxing for the mother. Of course, you must make sure the mother is in excellent health herself, or the newborns are not likely to survive and the mother will suffer as well.

When adding the orphans to an existing litter, before placing them in the nesting box with the other babies, rub the mother with a washcloth and then rub the washcloth on the new kitten or puppy. This will transfer her smell and increase the chances of her accepting them.

Monitor the situation, and if the mother will not accept the new orphans, you can remove her from the babies for about an hour. Give her a nice meal and perhaps some special one-on-one time. After about an hour, she will be anxious to get back to her litter, and by that point, all the babies should smell the same after they have scrambled all over each other. She may be more likely to accept the new ones at this point. Continue to monitor the situation. She may at first gently nudge away the new little ones, but some mothers will be aggressive and attack a foreign kitten or puppy. If this happens, do not try to reintroduce them. Proceed with bottle-feeding, and if you feel it may be safe, carefully try to reintroduce the baby at another time. Do not let a baby go more than two or three hours without feeding.

You may need to step in and give supplemental feedings and try to reintroduce them at a later time.

If you are adding a kitten or puppy to an existing litter, make sure all the babies are getting enough to eat. As good as a mother may be, she may not be able to produce enough milk. You can prepare a bottle and offer it to each baby every four to six hours, and the hungry babies will most likely accept the bottle. Do not assume that every member of a large litter is getting enough. Sometimes the runts will get pushed away, becoming increasingly weak and unable to get enough nourishment. You must step in and provide supplemental feedings, or they may die.

Facts About Newborn Kittens

- Newborn kittens generally weigh about three to five ounces at birth.

- Kittens are born blind and deaf. Their eyes will begin to open in about seven to fourteen days. They open gradually, usually starting to open from the nose outward. The eyes of short-haired cats will usually open earlier than the eyes of long-haired cats. The eyes of Siamese cats often open very early.

- All kittens have dark-blue eyes initially with no distinguished pupils. When kittens are about four to five weeks old, adult eye color will begin to appear, but it may not become its final color until nine to twelve weeks of age. At around four weeks old, kittens will begin to see fairly well, and their eyes will begin to look and function like an adult cat's eyes. They are developing visual depth perception, and their sight continues to improve through sixteen weeks.

- Kittens' ears begin to unfold when they are about two to three weeks old. Their hearing becomes progressively more sensitive as they grow older. Hearing is usually fully developed by the time kittens are three to five weeks old.

- A kitten's umbilical cord should drop off when it is about three to four days old.

- Testicles begin to become noticeable when kittens are around four weeks old.

Facts About Newborn Puppies

- A newborn puppy's average weight at birth depends on the breed. A Chihuahua puppy may weigh two ounces at birth while a Great Dane pup can weigh two pounds! In general, a puppy's weight should double in the first week of life.

- Puppies are born blind and deaf. Their eyes will begin to open in about ten to twelve days, but this may vary. They open gradually, usually starting to open from the nose outward.

- All puppies have grayish-blue eyes initially with no distinguished pupils. When puppies are about four weeks old, adult eye color will begin to appear, but it may not become its final color until about eight weeks of age. At around four weeks old, puppies will begin to see fairly well, and their eyes will begin to look and function like an adult dog's eyes. They are developing visual depth perception, and their sight continues to improve through ten weeks of age. In order to prevent damage, it is important for puppies to avoid bright lights until they reach six weeks old, as their eyes are developing.

- Puppies' ears begin to unfold when they are about two to three weeks old. Their hearing becomes progressively more sensitive as they grow older. They can usually hear sounds beginning at two to three weeks of age. Hearing is usually fully developed by the time puppies are about five weeks old.

- A puppy's umbilical cord should drop off when it is about three to four days old.

⚜ Testicles begin to become noticeable when they are around four weeks old.

Supplies You Will Need

Having supplies readily at hand and organized will be helpful when the call comes out of the blue for an animal that needs your help.

Supplies to have:

⚜ appropriate sizes of feeding tubes and nursing bottles

⚜ kitten or puppy replacement formula

⚜ different sizes and shapes of rubber nipples

⚜ cotton balls

⚜ safe heating source such as a SnuggleSafe® or heated bed specifically made for pets

⚜ mineral oil

⚜ stack of soft white cloths

⚜ small scale that weighs in ounces or grams

⚜ pediatric thermometer

⚜ lubricant

⚜ notebook and pen

⚜ gentle, all-natural skin balm

ᐁ warm bedding that is easily laundered

ᐁ a pet carrier or even a rodent cage to contain tiny babies

You may find that storing the small items in a plastic shoe box will help keep you organized.

Environment

It is very important to give thought ahead of time as to where you will house your tiny guests. Keeping them in a large bathroom has many advantages:

ᐁ With the door closed, they are isolated from other family pets. This is very important, as you will not know what disease or illness these babies may have been exposed to or may be carrying. This will also protect them from anything your own pets may be harboring.

ᐁ It is an easy space to keep warm.

ᐁ Generally, bathroom floors are easy to clean and disinfect.

ᐁ Water is readily available for washing hands, bathing animals, etc.

ᐁ It provides a quiet place for animals that need uninterrupted sleep.

Housing

For very young animals, a pet carrier is an ideal place to be contained. Carriers provide a safe place as well as good ventilation and the darkness that is required for good sleep.

Large rodent cages also work well for containing kittens or very small puppies. Covering the cage with a towel will help keep the babies warm and provide darkness needed for sleeping. If converting a used rodent cage, be sure to clean the cage thoroughly with dilute bleach and allow to air dry for one to two days before placing newborns in the cage.

Newborns cannot regulate their body temperature, so it is essential that you provide warmth in a safe manner. Keeping a newborn warm is very important. An animal that is cold may be unresponsive, will not be able to digest food, and may not survive. The ideal temperature is 85° to 90°F (29.4° to 32.2°C) during the first week. Decrease to 80°F to 72°F (26.7°C to 22.2°C) after the second week. If there are many kittens or puppies in the litter, the temperature can be slightly lower, as they will keep each other warm by huddling together.

To warm a chilled kitten or puppy:

- Warm slowly over one to two hours to a body temperature of 97-98°F (36.1-36.6°C).

- Wrap them in warm towels right out of the dryer.

- Place them inside a pet carrier on a SnuggleSafe or a heating pad made specifically for pets.

Even newborn animals have been noted moving toward a heat source. Conversely, you will also want an animal to be able to move away from heat. Make sure that the animal has an unheated area it can crawl to if too warm. When using a heating source under the carrier, place it under half of the carrier, thus leaving an unheated part for the animal to crawl to if it gets too warm.

An excellent choice for providing heat is a SnuggleSafe, a micro-wavable disc that retains heat for about eight hours. Placed under bedding, it provides heat that gradually lessens. This is preferable to using hot-water bottles, which may become cold and chill a young animal. Another excellent way to keep an animal consistently warm is a heated fleece bed. Take care to make sure the cord cannot be chewed on.

Be especially careful when using heat lamps, as they can burn or overheat newborns. Be careful if using electric heating pads, as they can either overheat, causing burns, or automatically turn off, leaving your newborn without a heat source.

Also, newborns require higher humidity than usual, which would have been provided by the presence of the mother. If there is no mother, try to keep humidity at 40 to 50 percent for the first two weeks. Keeping a humidifier in the room but away from the box is good. Do not place the humidifier too close to the nesting box, or it will mist the babies and chill them.

Feeding

Commercial Replacement Formulas

Commercial replacement formulas are an excellent way to ensure that you are giving complete and balanced nutrition to a newborn animal. There are several companies that make these. Kitten and puppy replacement formulas are not interchangeable—do not give puppy formula to a kitten and vice versa.

Formulas should be made strictly according to instructions and diluted with water if too thick. The formula should never be made more concentrated, as this may cause severe diarrhea. Any formula that is made (commercial or homemade) should be kept for twenty-four hours only and refrigerated. It should be discarded after twenty-four hours for new milk.

Colostrum

Colostrum is the nutrient-rich fluid secreted by all mammals near the time of giving birth. It is chock-full of immune and growth factors, vitamins, minerals, and amino acids. It is very important that newborn kittens and puppies nurse from the mother for the first twenty-four to forty-eight hours to receive colostrum. If this is not possible, contact your veterinarian about providing a supplement to provide antibody support. This may be in the form of the blood products plasma or serum or possibly a supplement made from bovine colostrum. If the neonates do not receive colostrum, they may not have a good immunity to common diseases and should be vaccinated early, at approximately six weeks.

Emergency Homemade Formulas

If a commercial formula is not available, here are several recipes you can use in a pinch. Please keep in mind that these milk recipes are very nutritionally unbalanced and should not be used for more than one or two days. In addition to the difference in proteins and fat, cow's milk is low in *arginine,* an essential amino acid, and the deficiency can cause cataracts when the newborns get older. Gradually switch to a commercial formula as soon as possible.

Goat's milk may be fed to kittens on a very temporary basis but should never be fed to puppies as it can cause severe constipation and even death. It is preferable to use cow's milk with puppies.

It is fine to use cow's milk in these recipes. Cats lose their ability to digest lactose when they are eight weeks old.

Kitten Recipe #1

½ cup (120 mL) whole milk
1 egg yolk
1 drop pediatric liquid vitamins

Kitten Recipe #2

½ cup (120 mL) evaporated milk
½ cup water
½ cup plain yogurt
3 to 4 egg yolks

Puppy Recipe

1 cup (240 mL) whole milk
1 tsp (5 mL) vegetable oil
1 drop pediatric liquid vitamins

Evaporated and condensed milk are the same thing. But do not use sweetened condensed or evaporated milk. It is normal that these types of milk are slightly darker. This is caused by high heat that is used in the evaporation process, causing the sugars to caramelize.

Do not use egg whites as they may cause diarrhea, or cottage cheese as it may form hard clots in the stomach and will not be digested.

How Often and How Much to Feed Kittens

There are many theories on the best way to feed orphan kittens. The following information is a good guideline as to what is successful.

A queen will nurse her kittens for about twenty hours a day. Newborn kittens or those under two weeks of age that are getting no milk from their mothers should be fed every two to three hours. Feed two- to four-week-old kittens every four to six hours. You can begin weaning to canned food at four weeks of age. Kittens should be fed periodically twenty-four hours a day when possible. Not feeding for prolonged periods causes poor weight gain, dehydration, and risk of aspiration as they feed more desperately after being fasted. Newborns can only ingest small amounts of food at a time and, if fasted overnight, may not be able to make up for the deficit during the day. Having said this, many kittens do fine sleeping through the night without being fed. Keep them close to you, as they will need to be fed if they wake up hungry. You will know this when they become fussy and start to cry. Well-fed kittens will continually gain weight, be sleepy and content after feeding, and have round tummies. An underfed kitten will feel scrawny, be weak and cranky, and may not survive.

Overfeeding may cause diarrhea, but that usually resolves once smaller feedings are given.

Determining how much to feed kittens depends on their age and weight. In general, commercial kitten milk replacement formulas will have guidelines on their labels for the proper amount to be fed and how often. Weighing the kittens is very important in determining the correct amount to be fed.

Feeding guidelines:

During weeks one and two, feed eight calories per ounce of body weight over a twenty-four-hour period.

During weeks three and four, feed seven calories per ounce of body weight over a twenty-four-hour period.

This amount should be split into meals appropriate for age. Always consult instructions on commercial milk replacers for amounts. Roughly, most kitten milk replacers, when diluted, correctly should provide roughly one calorie per mL.

For example:

A four-ounce kitten needs thirty-two calories per day.

If being fed kitten milk replacement (0.82 cal/ml), the kitten will need 39 ml per twenty-four hours, or 3 ml every two hours.

To figure out this amount: Multiply 4 (ounces) x 0.82 (calories per ml). This equals 39 ml to be fed over twenty-four hours. If you are feeding every two hours, divide this amount by twelve (amount of feedings per day).

How Often and How Much to Feed Puppies

Each litter of puppies is different, but here are general guidelines for feeding:

During week one, feed every two to three hours.

During week two, feed every four hours.

During week three, feed every five hours or so, and introduce solid food along with bottle-feedings.

As with kittens, many puppies will sleep through the night from the start and can be fed through the day only. Keep them close to you, as they will need to be fed if they wake up hungry. You will know this when they become fussy and start to cry. Well-fed puppies will continually gain weight, be sleepy and content after feeding, and have round tummies. An underfed puppy will feel scrawny, be cranky, and may not survive. Overfeeding may cause diarrhea, but that usually resolves once smaller feedings are given.

Determining how much to feed puppies depends on their age and weight. In general, commercial puppy milk replacement formulas will have guidelines on their labels for proper amounts to be fed and how often. Weighing the puppies is very important in determining the correct amount to be fed.

Feeding From a Nursing Bottle

Feeding a kitten or puppy from a nursing bottle is relatively easy, and most animals take to it quite readily. There is nothing as heartwarming as watching little ears wiggling as an animal is happily nursing from a bottle. Take care while bottle-feeding to give adequate nutrition and to use proper techniques to prevent problems.

Bottle-feeding basics:

- Do not feed a chilled animal. The milk will not be digested and will curdle in the stomach.

- Do not feed a weak or unconscious animal that cannot swallow. Forcing milk on an animal that is not swallowing properly can cause it to inhale the milk instead of swallowing. This is called aspiration.

- Only feed an appropriate nursing formula; do not feed cow's milk exclusively to kittens. Cow's milk is much lower in fat and protein and not adequate nutrition for kittens and puppies. Human infant formula is also not adequate nutrition for kittens and puppies.

- Do not let formula sit out when not in use. Do not use old or spoiled formula. Make sure to check expiration dates on all cans of liquid formula and canisters of powdered formula. Do not refrigerate and reuse formula that has been warmed up.

- Make sure the formula is warmed—not too hot or too cold. You can test a few drops on the inside of your wrist. It should feel slightly warm.

- If using powdered formula, make sure there are no lumps in the formula after mixing, or the formula may clog the nipple. Mix a small amount of powder into warm water and thoroughly mix before adding more powder. You can use a whisk, fork, or cup-size blender to mix the formula. Some people will mash the formula with the back of a spoon to break up the lumps before adding water. Another method is to put a measured amount of powdered formula and water in a small, clean, glass jar and shake it vigorously. Then use a tea strainer and pour the formula into another small glass jar. This catches any small lumps. The milk can also be stored in the jar.

- Make sure the nipple is an acceptable size and shape. There are several styles available, and you may have to experiment to see what the animal will accept. Nipples made for feeding orphaned squirrels are great for use with kittens. Using a longer nipple does increase the chances of aspiration, but some animals will use it more readily.

- Keep all supplies clean and sanitary by washing them in very warm, soapy water after *each* use. Rinse well with lots of water!

- Do not be in a hurry to feed animals. They need you to be patient and calm, as feeding may take some getting used to on both your parts.

- Gently wash any formula off the animal's fur after feeding. Bottle-fed babies must be kept clean.

- Bottle-fed babies may need to be gently burped. Burping them halfway through feeding can make them feel more comfortable and make room for the rest of the formula to be ingested.

- Bottle-fed babies need to be stimulated to urinate and defecate. (See below.)

- Weigh each animal before and after each feeding. Record the weights so there is no guessing if the animal is actually gaining weight or not. This will also help you know if you are feeding the correct amount.

Monitoring Weight

It is very important to monitor the weight of a nursing kitten or puppy. Early detection of failure to gain weight can help prevent deaths from poor nutrition and dehydration. Purchase a good kitchen or postal scale that measures in both ounces and grams.

The typical kitten birth weight is three to four ounces (90 to 110g). A normal, nursing kitten should gain about 1.8 to 3.5 ounces (50 to 100g) per week, or about 0.3 to 0.5 ounces (10 to 15 g) daily. They should double their birth weight by two weeks of age. It is common for kittens to lose 10 percent of their weight during the first twenty-four hours of life, but they should regain that weight quickly. Kittens should be weighed daily for the first two weeks to make sure they are gaining weight properly. Between two and four weeks, the kittens should be weighed every two days.

A healthy puppy should gain between 10 to 15 percent of its birth weight daily and should double its birth weight by the end of its second week. Puppies should be weighed daily. Large pups can be weighed on a human scale. First weigh yourself, and then weigh yourself and the puppy. Subtracting your weight from the total gives you the weight of the puppy.

Bottle-Feeding a Kitten or Puppy

Choose a quiet, warm place that is easy to clean. Bottle-feeding can be a little messy, especially if you are doing it for the first time. Newborn animals can be fed on a counter or tabletop, although many people like to sit on the floor and do this. Have on hand paper towels or small, damp washcloths for cleanup.

1. Warm the food using one of several methods. Formula should be about 102°F (38.9°C). You can microwave it in a small cup or bowl for a few seconds at a time, but be *very* careful not to burn the food. Stir constantly to prevent hot spots in the food. A preferred method is to measure out the amount to feed, put it in a small bowl, and put that bowl in a larger bowl with hot water, stirring every few seconds until it is warm enough to feed. This takes a little longer, but there is less danger of overheating. Another method of warming food is to place the bottles of food in a dish of very warm water. Make sure you don't let the water get chilly, therefore chilling the food.

2. Test the temperature of the food on the inside of your wrist (as you would test baby food) to make sure it is not too warm. Microwaving the food-filled bottles is not recommended, as you will not know how hot the food is inside the bottle. Microwaving may also destroy nutrients in the formula.

3. Place the kitten or puppy on a warm towel in a natural nursing position. A natural position when nursing from the mother is the kitten lying on its belly with its head slightly extended. Placing it on a warm towel will help it relax and stimulate it to suckle. Alternately, you can swaddle the kitten or puppy lightly in a warm towel, burrito-style. This may make it feel safe and secure, warm, and less frantic to be fed. Even if you do this, do not feed the animal tummy up, but instead position it to lean slightly forward.

4. Before introducing the nipple into the kitten or puppy's mouth, squeeze a little milk to moisten the nipple and to give the newborn the taste of milk. Gently open the animal's mouth and introduce the nipple. Place the nipple fully inside the mouth, taking care if it is a long nipple. Moving the nipple back and forth slightly will help stimulate the newborn to suck. To determine if the hole in the nipple is the proper size, hold the bottle upside down. You should see a slow drip of milk from the nipple. If the milk comes out in a stream, the hole is too large, and the milk may overwhelm the kitten or puppy, leading to aspiration.

5. Do not squeeze the nursing bottle, as it may introduce too much milk into the mouth. Milk getting into the lungs can be fatal.

6. A sign a kitten or puppy is nursing is when you see its ears wiggling. They may also knead with their front paws, or "make biscuits." This is what they do to stimulate the release of milk from their mother. Some kittens never outgrow this charming behavior and continue to do it as happy adults when on soft bedding or a soft lap!

7. Most babies will finish nursing in a few minutes and will become quiet, content, and sleepy when full.

8. Proceed to stimulate urination and defecation. See below.

Problems with bottle-feeding:

ᵔᵂ The level of milk stays the same in the bottle. If this happens, the baby is not getting any milk. This can be caused by the hole in the nipple being too small. You may need to slightly enlarge it. Also check to make sure the nipple is not clogged. You may also need to make sure there is not too much of a vacuum in the nursing bottle. This will make it difficult for the baby to suck and get milk. To fix this, unscrew the plastic collar on the bottle, allow air to return to the bottle, and then screw the collar back on.

ᵔᵂ The baby is getting too much milk, and it may be running out the corners of its mouth. The nipple or the hole in the nipple may be too large. Replace with a smaller nipple or a nipple with a smaller hole. Failure to do this may cause the baby to choke on the milk, as it cannot swallow it fast enough.

Tube-Feeding a Kitten or Puppy

There are times when tube-feeding is a much more practical and efficient way to feed a very young animal. Tube-feeding alleviates the worry of accidentally introducing milk into the lungs as can happen with a nursing bottle, syringe, or eyedropper. But it is vitally important to *place* the feeding tube correctly, or you will be introducing milk into the lungs.

Another advantage is that you can give the little one an exact amount of formula and can give a larger amount than with the feeding methods just mentioned. This also means less frequent feedings, which makes everyone happier!

Feeding tubes vary in size. For tiny kittens and puppies, a size 3.5 French red rubber feeding tube works well. It is very thin, flexible, and easy to insert. Larger puppies and kittens could comfortably accommodate a size 5 French feeding tube. Your veterinarian will give you advice as to the appropriate size to use.

The words *gently* and *slowly* cannot be overused when describing this process! Do not rush through this procedure. Make sure your supplies are all close at hand and ready to go.

Feeding tube basics:

- Ask veterinary advice on determining the correct size tube to use. *You can seriously injure a newborn animal by using too large a tube.*

- Ask for a lesson from a veterinary technician or someone knowledgeable in tube-feeding.

- Follow instructions carefully, especially if this is your first time doing this. Tiny babies are very fragile, and there is not much room for error.

- Make sure all feeding tubes and syringes are kept clean and sanitary by washing in very warm, soapy water after each use. Rinse well with lots of water!

- Weigh each animal before and after each feeding. Record the weights so there is no guessing if the animal is actually gaining weight. This will also help you know if you are feeding the correct amount.

You will need:

- An assistant, at least for the first time

- An appropriate size of soft rubber feeding tube

- A permanent marker

꙰ Warmed formula appropriate for the animal you are feeding

꙰ A soft, warm, damp washcloth

꙰ A small scale—postage or dietary scales work well for very small animals

꙰ Pen and paper for recording the animal's name, feeding time, weight, and amount of formula given. You may also want to make notes about the animal's condition, behavior, etc.

Steps for Tube-Feeding a Kitten or Puppy

If you accidently place the feeding tube into the trachea (windpipe) instead of the esophagus, you will deliver milk into the lungs. *If you are unsure of doing the correct placement, do not proceed.* It is always best to have someone demonstrate this procedure for you.

1. You will need to measure the correct length for the feeding tube. This is very important, so have someone help you by holding the kitten or puppy. Practice first, and feel the location of the last rib on the animal. The rib you want to feel is the one closest to the tail. While your helper holds the animal, place the tube, with the smaller tube opening toward the tail (see picture), against the animal's body and measure from the tip of the nose to this rib. Mark the tube with permanent marker at that spot. You will do this so you know how far to put the tube into the animal. Failing to put the tube deep enough and not into the stomach can cause regurgitation if the formula is delivered into the esophagus.

2. Weigh the baby, and record the weight. Calculate the correct amount to be fed. Recheck your calculations to make sure you are not giving too much or too little. This is very important.

3. Draw this amount up into the syringe from the container of warmed formula. Check the temperature of the formula by putting several drops on the inside of your wrist to make sure it is neither too warm nor too cold.

4. Attach the tube to the end of the syringe. Slowly depress the plunger until a small amount of formula comes out of the end of the feeding tube. Dip the tube into the container of formula. This lubricates and encourages the baby to swallow the tube.

5. Hold the baby in a natural nursing position. A natural nursing position is how the animal would be positioned while nursing from its mother. It is not lying on its back!

6. Very gently support the back of the animal's head and open the mouth by pulling down the lower jaw with the tip of your middle finger. Tip the head back and begin to insert the tube over the center of the tongue and into the throat. Expect this to feel awkward at first. But with time and practice, you should be able to complete this with no assistance. If the tube does not go in easily, you may be introducing it into the trachea instead of the esophagus. *Do not force the tube in; seek veterinary advice.*

7. Continue to slowly pass the tube until you reach the mark on the feeding tube. If you meet any resistance, gently withdraw the tube and begin again. If this is the first time you have done this, and you are still not able to pass the tube to the marked spot, seek veterinary advice. Once you are sure the tube is in place, attach the syringe with formula to the end of the tube, and slowly depress the plunger on the syringe to deliver the formula. *Do not deliver the formula if the tube is not correctly in place or if you are unsure if it is.* The food should be pushed in slowly over ten minutes. Feeding too fast will make the stomach expand too quickly, causing cramping and pain and increasing the chance of vomiting.

8. Once you have given the entire amount, you may slowly remove the feeding tube.

Stimulating an Animal to Urinate and Defecate

Part of playing mama to a newborn is helping it to eliminate its own waste. By licking the baby's abdomen and under the tail, the mother stimulates the bowels and bladder and cleans up the resulting mess. Doing this helps the newborn to eliminate toxins (waste products), helps it to stay clean, and also helps the nest stay clean. *After each feeding, the newborn must be stimulated to urinate and defecate.* Gently rubbing the little one's abdomen will help it to relax, and rubbing its genitals and anal region with a warm cotton ball or tissue will stimulate it to urinate or defecate. Do not worry if your newborn animal does not defecate each time. Gentle *rubbing* will stimulate the newborn to begin eliminating, and gentle *dabbing* will help it keep eliminating. Even tiny kittens can produce a good amount of urine, so hold your newborn over a litter box, absorbent pad, or something to contain the flow of urine. Keep the area clean, and watch for irritation, which might indicate that you are rubbing too hard or not cleaning well enough. It will be necessary for you to continue to stimulate the newborn until it can eliminate on its own, usually at three weeks of age for kittens. This time varies in puppies. Often, when an animal gets fussy when you are stimulating it, it may be on its way to eliminating on its own. Any animal that does not defecate for more than two days should be checked by a veterinarian.

It is also recommended to stimulate the newborn to urinate or defecate, or both, before feeding. This will relieve the animal of what it is holding from the previous meal and make it more comfortable with being handled.

After three weeks or so, the process of litter box training can begin. A good method is to use a flat cardboard box that has an absorbent pad in it and a handful of recycled newspaper pellets as scratching material. Place a kitten in the box, take its paw, and do a gentle scratching motion in the pellets. You may need to do this repeatedly until the kitten gets the idea. You can also use inexpensive unscented clay litter, but never clumping litter. Tiny kittens can ingest clumping litter and this can be harmful. Set the kittens in the litter box before and after eating and, again, remind them what to do by using their paws to scratch in the litter. Many will do this instinctively at a young age while some need to learn this. Check the kittens' bedding throughout the day as they may dribble urine or get feces on it.

There are several theories on the best way to potty train a puppy. You can find great information from your veterinary team, dog trainers, online, or in books devoted to the subject.

Weaning Kittens

Kittens can be offered solid food when they are around four weeks old. This is not to replace bottle milk at this point but as an introduction. Start with quality canned kitten food, and offer them a small bit on your finger. Let them smell the food first, and then gently place a tiny piece on the kittens' tongues. But be careful of tiny kitten teeth—they are very sharp! Make sure they swallow that before offering more. You can mix a little bottle formula into the canned food to give it a familiar taste, although some kittens prefer to eat solid food when moistened only with warm water. Some kittens will eat more of the food if it is chunky, as they may be better able to take small bites of it. You may need to experiment to see what each kitten prefers. Gradually, kittens should eat more and more of this food and by five weeks old should be able to eat the canned food gruel from a plate. Expect that the kittens will walk all over the plate of food and get quite messy. It may be difficult to figure out how much of the food has actually been eaten and how much is being worn. During the weaning process, continue to weigh the kittens to make sure they are gaining weight. Do not discontinue bottle-feeding until you are certain the kittens are ingesting most of the food. By six weeks old, kittens should be off the bottle and consuming dry kibble and canned food. Offer canned food two to three times daily, and remove what is not eaten in thirty minutes. A kitten should have access to a high-quality kibble that is labeled for kittens and is approved by the Association of American Feed Control Officials (AAFCO). You can find the certification for this near the list of ingredients on the label. At this point, the kittens must also have access to fresh water at all times. Kittens should gain about a pound a month from now on, at least for the first 4-5 months. Bear in mind, weight gain can vary. If you have any questions or concerns about the kittens weight gain (or lack of) consult with your veterinarian.

Weaning puppies

When puppies are three weeks old, you can introduce them to eating from a dish. This is to supplement bottle-feeding, not to replace it. Mix canned puppy food with the milk replacer to make a thick gruel. The mixture should not be too thick or too thin. Warming the food slightly will encourage them to eat it, as it will smell stronger. Let them smell the food first, and then put a small bit on your finger or gently place a tiny piece on the puppies' tongues. Puppies' teeth are very sharp, so please be careful! Expect that the puppies will walk all over the plate of food and get quite messy. It may be difficult to figure out how much of the food has actually been eaten and how much is being worn. So do not discontinue bottle-feeding until you are certain the puppies are ingesting most of the food. In time, gradually decrease the amount of milk replacer in the gruel. By four to five weeks old, the puppies should be off the bottle and consuming dry kibble and canned food. Offer canned food two to three times daily, and remove what is not eaten in thirty minutes. A puppy should have access to a high-quality kibble that is labeled for puppies and is approved by the Association of American Feed Control Officials (AAFCO). You can find the certification for this near the list of ingredients on the label. Puppies must also have access to fresh water at all times. By four to four-and-a-half weeks, the puppy should consume enough moistened solid food to meet its nutritional needs.

Suckling Behavior of Kittens and Puppies

Occasionally, in some litters there are puppies or kittens that will nurse on each other, usually around the genitals. While this is normal behavior, it can cause skin irritation and swelling. One solution is to offer the bottle more often to these babies in the hope of satisfying their need to suck. Another solution to this problem is to separate them from the litter as needed, but it is very important to put them together, supervised, as often as possible. It is important that they be allowed to be with the rest of the litter for socialization and for them to learn play behavior. The use of aversives, such as a foul-tasting liquid, to discourage sucking is generally not recommended in very young animals. Many animals will grow out of this behavior, but some kittens may continue it as adults, often wanting to suck on their guardians' earlobes.

How to Tell the Sex of Kittens and Puppies

It is not easy, even for experienced kitten caretakers, to determine the sex of very young animals.

To check the sex, hold up the baby so that it is facing away from you, and hold up its tail. In both male and female kittens, the anus is the opening just under the tail. Below the anus is the genital opening. This opening is round in males and is a vertical slit in females. The distance between the anus and the genital opening is shorter in the female than the male. In male kittens, the space is longer to because this is where the testicles will drop down from the body cavity and into the scrotal sacs as they get older. After about 4 to 6 weeks of age, the testicles can be felt in the scrotal sacs. They feel like tiny round objects in the space between the anus and penis.

It is often easier to hold up two babies to see if you can tell a difference in anatomy that indicates if they are in fact male and female.

The fur color of a kitten can also give clues to its gender. Calico (black, orange, and white) or tortoiseshell (black and orange) cats are almost always (98 percent) females. Most, but not all, orange kittens are male.

If it is still not easy to tell the sex, just know that testicles get larger and become more noticeable with time. There are also excellent pictures online to help you distinguish the sex of your kittens or puppies.

Health Concerns of Kittens and Puppies

In general, kittens and puppies are hardy babies, but there are several health concerns of which you should be aware. As always, your veterinarian is the best source of medical advice on their health. Ask them if you have any concerns about the health of your newborns. The rest of this chapter describes some health concerns.

Panleukopenia

Two closely related diseases with different names can quickly strike puppies and kittens. The disease that affects cats and kittens is feline panleukopenia virus (FPV), also called feline infectious enteritis and commonly known as feline distemper. (Distemper is not an accurate name, though, as the disease is closely related to canine parvovirus, not canine distemper.) Dogs and puppies are affected by canine parvovirus (CPV). The meaning of the word panleukopenia is basically an overall lack of white blood cells. Blood work and characteristic physical signs are a very accurate way of diagnosing this disease.

Panleukopenia and parvovirus both affect the intestinal tract, causing pain and a distinctive bloody and foul-smelling diarrhea. There is no cure, although providing supportive care can be successful in saving the kitten or puppy's life. It is a highly deadly virus that strikes quickly, causing death in only a few hours. It is also extremely contagious. These viruses are spread from animal to animal through contact with an infected animal's bodily fluids and feces, as well as through contact with an infected animal's toys, bedding, or food dishes. Additionally, the virus can spread by contact with the clothing and shoes of anyone handling infected animals. Some animals contract the virus from an infected mother when they are in the womb.

The virus has an incubation period of two to fourteen days. Cats and kittens are thought to be contagious two to three days before the first symptoms appear, and they may spread the disease for four to six weeks after appearance of the first symptoms.

Feline distemper and canine parvovirus are very hardy and can live in the environment for a year. It is very resistant to common disinfectants, although bleach is effective in killing the virus.

To prevent spread of disease, it is best to discard the infected animal's food dishes, bedding, and toys. These items, along with the floor and cages, may also be disinfected with bleach and water diluted at 1:32 (one-half cup bleach per gallon of water).

Signs of distemper and parvovirus:

- Vomiting

- High fever

- Anorexia

- Lethargy

- Dehydration

- Diarrhea

- Lack of muscular coordination

- Sudden death

One characteristic sign of the virus in a kitten is that it becomes dehydrated and very thirsty, often sitting or hanging its head over a water bowl. If you see this or another sign, please *seek veterinary advice as soon as possible.*

Supportive care generally involves treating dehydration with subcutaneous (SC) or intravenous (IV) fluids and may include antibiotics and medication to control vomiting and diarrhea.

Kittens that are infected with feline distemper before birth and survive may have cerebellar hypoplasia. This is the result of the virus attacking part of the brain, the cerebellum, and affecting its development. This may also occur if the mother was vaccinated during a pregnancy with certain vaccines. The cerebellum is responsible for coordinating movements and maintaining balance and equilibrium. *Cerebellar hypoplasia* (CH) can cause animals to walk with an uncoordinated motion, be wobbly, and in extreme cases not be able to walk. This is not a progressive condition, and some cats learn to compensate well. In the right homes, these animals can lead long and healthy lives. Care must be taken to ensure that they cannot hurt themselves, have a good quality of life, and are kept out of harm's way.

Diarrhea and Constipation

The consistency of the newborn's stool is very important. You may notice stool that has a good shape or it may be slightly loose diarrhea, or may be completely liquid. Ideally, it should be able to keep its shape when deposited. Having blood in the stool is not normal. Diarrhea can be caused by intestinal parasites, a virus, overfeeding, or an incorrect nutritional balance in the food.

In otherwise healthy animals that are still being bottle-fed, you may first try diluting the milk replacer by 50 percent with water for twenty-four hours or switching to an oral electrolyte solution such as Pedialyte® for a few meals to help with dehydration. The stool should become more formed within twenty-four hours.

If the kitten or puppy has been weaned and is on canned food, you can also add cooked barley, white rice, or its liquid to the regular canned food. You may also add Fortiflora® or other probiotics to the food to help rebalance the normal intestinal bacterial flora after diarrhea.

Kaolin/pectin preparations are often sold over the counter and are safe when given as directed to otherwise healthy puppies and kittens with simple diarrhea. The preparations may also mask symptoms and are best used only for a few days.

If the kitten or puppy is becoming lethargic or stops eating, have it checked by a veterinarian immediately. Newborn animals will become dehydrated extremely quickly and may require fluids.

If there is no improvement, have your veterinarian check a stool sample. Even if diarrhea is not present, this is a very good idea. Worms or an overgrowth of bacteria can be causes for diarrhea. Puppies and kittens are routinely dewormed even when worms are not suspected and diarrhea is not present. Having the sample checked will allow your veterinarian to dispense an appropriate dewormer or antibiotic if necessary. Kittens and puppies can be dewormed as early as two weeks of age with a safe medication prescribed by a veterinarian.

If diarrhea develops, be extremely careful to monitor for irritation of the skin. The kitten or puppy should be cleaned whenever it has diarrhea and dried thoroughly to prevent a drop in body temperature. Ointments such as Aquaphor or an all-natural healing balm should be used on any irritated skin.

Alternatively, constipation can develop in kittens or puppies that are not receiving enough fluids. If they are not producing bowel movements easily when stimulated, or if they have hard stools, try diluting the milk replacer by one-fourth to one-third with water. You can also stimulate them to defecate more easily by rubbing their anuses with cotton swabs dipped in mineral oil. This will also provide lubrication for drier stools and make them easier to pass. Mineral oil should never be added to bottle milk because if even only a few drops are aspirated, it can prove to be fatal to a neonatal puppy or kitten.

Internal Parasites

Kittens and puppies are at risk of having internal parasites such as roundworms, hookworms, coccidia, and giardia. Tapeworms may not be present at such an early age. Roundworms are a very common internal parasite of puppies and kittens and are often passed from the mother. Roundworms may look disturbing (they look like small pieces of spaghetti) in vomit or feces, but they are very easily treated with the appropriate dewormer. Coccidia is a more serious concern and is suspected whenever an animal has very yellow diarrhea. If you see this, seek veterinary care at once, as kittens and puppies can get sick very quickly and may die if left untreated. Giardia can often be difficult to diagnose and may require multiple fecal checks by a veterinarian but is treatable.

External Parasites

External parasites such as fleas and lice can also be present on a kitten or puppy. Because fleas feast on an animal's blood, it is very important to control them. A flea comb can be used, as many animals are too young to be treated with other flea products. Failing to control fleas can result in an anemic animal that may not survive. Ask your veterinarian for recommendations about what can be used safely. *NEVER* use over-the-counter flea products on any animal, especially sick or newborn animals, without consulting with your veterinarian. Lice are often found on sickly puppies, kittens, and elderly, debilitated animals. They can be easily and safely treated with an appropriate flea product such as Frontline.

Fungal Infections

Kittens and puppies can suffer from fungal skin infections such as ringworm. Ringworm is not a worm but a fungal infection that causes red, round, scaly patches on the skin. See Chapter 9.

Eye Infections

Newborns can suffer from eye infections such as *conjunctivitis*. This is an inflammation of the conjunctiva and what we refer to as pinkeye. The conjunctiva is a mucous membrane, just like the lining of the mouth and nose. These membranes consist of a layer of cells that secrete mucus. Most animals (except for human and pigs) have a third eyelid, or nictitating membrane, in the inner corner of the eye. The third eyelid is also covered by conjunctiva.

Often, conjunctivitis is in combination with an upper respiratory infection. The kitten or puppy will have yellow discharge from the nose and eyes. It is very important to keep the nose clean as much as possible. If the animal is unable to breathe through its nose, it will also not be willing to eat since it cannot smell its food.

The causes of conjunctivitis and upper respiratory infections are typically viral or bacterial. In newborns, one cause is from bacteria (chlamydia) that are transmitted from the infected mother's birth canal. If the infection has spread from the mother, the conjunctivitis will become noticeable when the newborn is ten to fourteen days old and the eyes seem to bulge out. Often, the upper and lower eyelids will be stuck together.

Other frequent causes include viruses, such as herpes or calici virus. If you suspect your newborn is developing a respiratory infection, a visit to a veterinarian is recommended to make sure that it can breathe well and that no pneumonia is present.

Conjunctivitis and upper respiratory infections are highly contagious to all animals in the litter.

Until you can get veterinary care, you can:

- Very gently place a warm, damp towel over the eyes. You can also use a cotton ball soaked with a sterile eye irrigation solution or saline solution if possible. Do not use contact lens solution. This may help draw the pus away from the eyes and keep them clear. Do not try to pry the eyelids open.

Failure to treat eye infections can cause permanent eye damage, including blindness.

Failure to Thrive

It is true that despite all your loving attention and proper care, a kitten or puppy may not survive. Sometimes it happens quite suddenly and for no apparent reason. Congenital abnormalities (such as a heart problem or poor development of the brain or GI tract), poor prior nutrition, illness, overwhelming parasites, or stress are all reasons a young animal may not make it. It is the nature of caring for these tiny animals that sometimes the weakest ones people worry about the most do fine, while ones that seemed hardy and healthy suddenly take a turn for the worst.

Kittens may suffer from Fading Kitten Syndrome (FKS). FKS is a general term used when kittens fade away and die after several days or weeks of seemingly good health. There are some possible causes, although no one knows for sure. Various bacteria, viruses, or a mismatch in the mother' and kitten's blood types are all thought to be possible causes. Some kittens may fail to thrive from birth although they seem to suckle normally. Others will appear to be doing fine and then slowly fade away.

Sadly, even with early veterinary intervention and aggressive measures to save a newborn's life, treatment may not be successful. In such young and tender babies, the treatment required to try to save them is invasive, costly, and most often unsuccessful. For these reasons, many people make the decision to let them pass gently on their own unless suffering is apparent. Most often, a failing puppy or kitten will quietly pass into unconsciousness, followed by an uneventful death.

You will know that a kitten or puppy is heading toward death when you notice the following:

- lethargy, weakness, stumbling, falling over, or inability to walk

- refusal to eat

- gasping for breath

- crying out (when others in the litter are quiet)

- coma

The best thing to do is to keep the animal with the littermates or mother, to keep it warm and comfortable. If you choose, call your veterinary office to set up an appointment for an exam for the newborn and to discuss what treatment options are available.

Vaccinating Kittens and Puppies

Kittens and puppies are provided some immunity to diseases by the mother's antibodies. Antibodies are a type of protein produced in a certain type of white blood cell. Simply put, the function of antibodies is to identify and fight off foreign invaders such as bacteria and viruses. Some antibodies cross the placenta and enter into the animal's bloodstream. The majority of maternal antibodies are provided in the colostrum. Kittens and puppies are only able to absorb the colostrum from the mother in the first two days of life, which is why it is important for them to nurse from their own mother for the first day. These maternal antibodies can help protect the kittens and puppies against diseases to which the mother is immune.

Depending on the strength of the mother's immunity, the maternal antibodies last for four to ten weeks; after this time, the kitten or puppy becomes susceptible to disease. A series of vaccines are recommended, as the maternal antibiotics may interfere with the kitten or puppy's response to the vaccine. Talk to your veterinarian about the recommended time to schedule first vaccinations.

Don't forget—even if you cannot take on the responsibilities of adopting a kitten or puppy, humane societies and rescue groups always need foster parents. Now is a great time to put your loving heart and skills to work!

ༀ

CHAPTER 15
Advanced Care Procedures

What you will learn in this chapter:

ண How to care for bandages and casts

ண When to express a pet's bladder

ண How to collect fecal and urine samples

ண When pets can benefit from physical therapy

ண How to weigh your pet

Nursing care for pets can range from providing a few days of TLC and special foods to learning new skills such as bandaging, giving subcutaneous fluids, and even doing physical therapy.

You don't need to have nursing experience to learn skills that can greatly enhance your pet's quality of life. These skills may enable your pet to spend more time at home and less time in the hospital when recovering from an illness, injury, or surgery. Your veterinary team can teach you these skills, while you supply the patience and a desire to learn. If you are unable to do what your pet may need, a veterinary technician or skilled pet sitter may be available to come to your home to assist you.

Bandage and Cast Care

Bandages, casts, and splints are applied when a pet has an injury that needs support or protection. It is very important that you check them at least twice daily. It is also important to keep your pet in a clean and dry environment when it is wearing a bandage or cast.

Ask your veterinarian for specific instructions on changing your pet's bandages. Taking a pet first aid class can also teach you this valuable skill. For more information, visit www.redcross.org.

Here are some basic concepts concerning the care of bandages:

- A bandage must be kept clean and dry. It is very important that dirt, bacteria, and moisture stay out of the wound. Whenever possible, keep your pet inside. If your pet has a cast or splint, you may need to restrict its movements by confining it in a crate or small area. (For more information on crate rest, see Chapter 3.)

- When taking your dog outside for potty breaks or short walks, place a plastic bag over the bandaged area, cast, or splint. Empty bread bags and IV solution bags work well if they are clean and dry on the inside. It is also very important to remove the plastic covering within an hour to prevent moisture from building up inside the plastic bag.

- Check the bandage twice daily for any signs of blood, discharge, or foul odor.

- Before taking your pet home from the veterinary hospital, note the position of the bandage, cast, or splint. Often, they will slip or move slightly even with normal movement. Changes in the position may cause skin irritation and interfere with healing.

- Check the toes twice daily if visible. You need to monitor them for swelling and redness. If the toes feel excessively warm or cold, report this to your veterinarian as soon as possible.

- Make sure your pet is not chewing on the bandage, cast, or splint. See Chapter 1 for information on e-collars and Chapter 11 for how to discourage chewing on bandages.

- Follow your veterinarian's instructions for when to have rechecks and appointments for removing the bandage, cast, or splint. Schedule them in a timely manner.

- Try to keep your pet from slipping while wearing a bandage, cast, or splint. Use area rugs, bath mats, or yoga mats to provide traction.

If you have any concerns about your pet's bandage, cast, or splint, contact your veterinarian as soon as possible. Failure to do so can cause further damage or delay healing.

Expressing a Pet's Bladder

Manually emptying your cat or dog's bladder is called expressing the bladder. Different conditions or injuries can cause an animal to not be able to void urine and empty its bladder. Many people learn to do this procedure so they can do it at home, as most animals will tolerate it quite well. The place to learn to do this is not in a book or on the Internet but in your veterinarian's office. By doing it wrong, you will be unsuccessful, and you may also cause injury to your pet.

A pet's bladder needs to be completely emptied at least every eight hours if possible, although some animals will still dribble or leak urine. Expressing the bladder completely helps to prevent infection as it prevents urine from staying in the bladder too long and creating an environment where bacteria can flourish. It also prevents an *atonic* bladder, a large, stretched urinary bladder that does not empty. The stretched bladder can become a chronic condition, and the pet may be unable to urinate normally even after bladder control returns.

Consult your veterinarian if:

- Your pet's urine seems dark, cloudy, bloody, or pink-tinged

- Your pet's urine has a foul or fishy smell

- Your pet seems uncomfortable or in pain when you express its bladder

- You are not able to fully express the bladder

- The skin around your pet's penis or urinary opening is red, irritated, or inflamed

Seek veterinary care at once if the bladder seems hard or full and you are unable to express any urine.

Often, fecal matter will be released as the bladder is being expressed. This is normal. When this happens, take care to make sure no fecal matter remains on the skin or fur.

How to Collect Fecal Samples

The fecal sample you bring to your veterinarian should be as fresh as possible. You can refrigerate a fecal sample up to about eight hours. Do not use a sample that is over twenty-four hours old. A dried-out sample will be of no use when testing. If the sample is very soft or liquid, do your best to scoop up enough to be tested. A disposable plastic spoon works well to scoop up a soft fecal sample.

Keep in mind that many animals will defecate shortly after they eat. It may be possible to get a fresh sample by timing your pet's meal.

Cats: You may have to be especially vigilant about cleaning the litter box so you know the sample you collect is the freshest one.

It is OK if the sample has some litter on it. The fecal sample should be about a tablespoon or two. You can put it in a clean, empty pill vial, plastic bag, yogurt container, baby food jar, or other clean container.

Dogs: An easy way to collect a fecal sample from a dog is to cover your hand with a plastic bag and to collect the sample with your bagged hand. (You may want to "double bag"!) Collect a sample that is about two tablespoons, and turn the bag inside out and knot it. Place this in a second bag or container. You can also use a disposable spoon or a tongue depressor to collect the sample.

How to Obtain Urine Samples From a Cat

You can use the following methods to obtain a urine sample to bring to your veterinarian or to test your diabetic cat's urine to see if it contains glucose. If you are testing at home with glucose reagent strips, you can also place the reagent strip in the flow of urine if you are lucky enough to get there at the right time!

Method #1

1. Start with a clean litter box that has been washed and *thoroughly* rinsed with a lot of fresh water.

2. Add nonabsorbent litter pearls, clean and rinsed aquarium gravel, plastic beads, or a product called No-Sorb® that is available from veterinarians.

3. You may have to separate your cats if you have more than one, so you know exactly which one used the box.

4. Once you have urine in the box, pour it (and the collection material) into a *clean and rinsed* jar or container. You can also collect the urine with a syringe to use with a reagent strip or transfer to a container. If taking the sample to your vet, try to get the sample

there as soon as possible. You can refrigerate it if needed for a short time.

Method #2

1. Start with a clean litter box; place your cat's normal cat litter in it.

2. Slip a clear or white trash bag over the whole thing. Note: You may want to trim your cat's nails the day before you do this, so it does not shred the bag.

3. Once you have urine in the box, gently remove the plastic bag and carefully pour the urine into a *clean and rinsed* jar or container. You can also collect the urine with a syringe to use with a reagent strip or transfer to a container. If taking the sample to your vet, try to get the sample there as soon as possible. You can refrigerate it if needed for a short time.

Method #3

1. Offer your cat a *clean*, empty litter box.

2. Once it has urinated, follow the directions for collection as above.

Method #4

Another excellent product to use is the Breeze® litter box system by Tidy Cat. This system uses nonabsorbent pellets in a slotted litter tray. When the cat urinates in it, the urine is collected in a tray underneath, which contains an absorbent pad. To obtain a urine sample, thoroughly clean the tray (it slides out completely), replace it under the box, but *do not* replace the absorbent pad. After the cat urinates in the box, you can pour the urine from the tray into a clean container or use a syringe to remove it.

Cats often like to use a freshly cleaned litter box. After you have set up the litter box with the method of your choice, put your cat next to it or in it. You may be surprised at how quickly you get your sample.

Checking urine for glucose:

1. Offer your cat a clean litter box with plain clay (not clumping) litter in it

2. Once your cat urinates in it, take a scoop of the saturated litter and add a little water to it. Test this liquid for glucose using a glucose dipstick. This will give you a result that is positive or negative for glucose in the urine.

How to Obtain Urine Samples From a Dog

1. Choose a time that your dog normally urinates or watch for its signals that its time to go. Some dogs will signal by becoming restless, moving toward the door, or vocalizing.

2. Use a flat container such as a pie tin or plastic food container to collect the urine. After your pet has started urinating, put the container into the stream of urine. For dogs that are low to the ground, attaching this container to a handle may make it easier. You might try a broom handle, plant stake, ruler, or yardstick.

3. If you are not successful the first time (some animals can be suspicious), wait until your pet really has to go, perhaps in another hour or so.

4. Once the urine is collected, pour it into a *clean and rinsed* jar or container. You can also collect the urine with a syringe to use with a urine glucose reagent strip or transfer to a container. If taking the sample to your vet, try to get the sample there as soon as possible. You can refrigerate it if needed for a short time.

Physical Therapy

As with human beings, physical therapy can be very beneficial for animals in many different situations. Never start a physical therapy program without consulting with your veterinarian.

Physical therapy may be useful for the pet who:

- Is recovering from injury, trauma, or surgery

- Has neurological problems

- Has mobility issues, chronic pain, or stiffness

- Is paralyzed

An initial consultation with a veterinarian who is trained in physical therapy includes a physical exam, a neurological exam, and often a gait analysis. Based on these findings, a plan will be structured for your pet. Many people learn to do physical therapy exercises at home. Patience is needed throughout the course of treatment as progress may be slow, and physical therapy needs to be done at the rate your pet can tolerate. Neurologically, an animal can only do as much as its nerves can accept, as healing can be very slow. Occasionally, daily exercise is needed for a successful treatment.

Some possible treatments include:

- Applying hot and cold packs

- Hydrotherapy (water therapy)

- Stretching

- Treadmills

- Ultrasound

- Massage

- Laser therapy

- Passive range-of-motion exercises

Some possible benefits of physical therapy include:

- Increasing mobility, endurance, agility, and flexibility

- Reducing pain and lowering dose of or need for pain medication

- Helping with safe weight loss

- Increasing muscle strength

- Conditioning athletic or working dogs to prevent injury

- Reducing stress

- Supporting recovery from injury

Pets on crate rest can often benefit from passive range-of-motion exercises, massage, and exercise to stimulate circulation. Because different animals have different needs, it is important to seek veterinary advice before starting your pets on any of these therapies.

Hydrotherapy (water exercise) is an excellent way for a pet to regain flexibility and muscle strength even when it cannot bear weight on its legs or when it has balance problems. Hydrotherapy can be done in a bathtub, hot tub, pool, or lake. Some veterinary hospitals have excellent facilities for dogs to swim safely. Some people even buy flotation devices (life jackets) for their pets and do therapy at home. Again, do not undertake this therapy without veterinary advice.

Weighing Your Pet

As part of monitoring, weighing your pet weekly (not more often) can help you spot trends in weight gain or loss. If weight loss is the goal, make sure you understand your vet's guidelines. Losing weight too fast can cause serious medical problems.

In cats, a fluctuation of two to three pounds over the course of a month or two is very significant. It is thought that cats should lose no more than 1 to 2 percent of their body weight per month. For more information, please read Dr. Lisa Pierson's excellent advice at www.catinfo.org. Because of the difference in the size of dogs, similar fluctuations in dogs should also be investigated. It may be difficult to spot weight loss in fluffy or long-haired cats and dogs, so periodic weighing can help you spot a weight loss trend before it becomes significant.

A small pet can be weighed just by holding it while you stand on a bathroom scale. You will then need to reweigh yourself without the pet and subtract the difference. You can also use a baby or small-pet scale for pets under thirty pounds.

For larger dogs, ask your vet if you can take your dog into the office for periodic weigh-ins. This is also a good way to desensitize a dog that may be nervous when going to the vet's office. Turn it into a fun time by using positive interaction, which may include petting, gentle scratching, and a healthy treat given by a member of the veterinary staff.

As always, your veterinary team is your best source of medical information. Never hesitate to ask questions about any part of your pet's medical care. Your furry friend depends on you to do your very best!

CHAPTER 16
Pet First Aid

What you will learn in this chapter:

- What some pet first aid basics are

- How to treat abscesses

- How to stop bleeding

- How to recognize blood sugar (glucose) problems

- What cardiopulmonary resuscitation (CPR) is

- How to check if a cat or dog is breathing

- How to check a cat or dog for a pulse

- How to do rescue breathing

- How to use acupuncture to stimulate respiration

- What an alternative CPR technique is

- How to check gum color and capillary refill time (CRT)

- What chocolate toxicity is

- How to handle cold-related emergencies

- How to handle heat-related emergencies

- How to treat simple diarrhea

- What seizures are and what to do if your pet has one

- What TPR is—temperature, pulse, respiration

- How to take care of wounds

- When and how to induce vomiting

- How to assemble a pet first aid kit

Taking a pet first aid class can be tremendously helpful for anyone taking care of pets and especially for those in outlying areas not served by veterinarians or veterinary emergency clinics. Check with your local humane society or Red Cross to see if there are any classes in your area. You can also buy pet first aid guides. The American Red Cross publishes an excellent guide that includes helpful information as well as an educational DVD.

Training in pet first aid teaches you not only how to act but also how to react. Animal lovers' instincts often are to rush in to help any animal needing help, but thought must be given to how to do this appropriately and safely.

Pet First Aid Basics

- Always be careful while approaching an ill or injured animal, even if it is your own. Animals may bite or scratch out of fear, pain, or if confused and disoriented. Watch for warning signals such as growling, hissing, ears pressed back, hair standing up along the back, baring teeth, or dilated pupils. But keep in mind that some animals will give no warning before striking out. Use precautions to safely restrain an animal before attempting to treat or help it.

- Remember that pets can easily pick up on people's feelings and emotions. Take a deep breath, and proceed as calmly as you can. They need you to think clearly and take appropriate action, not to panic.

- Do not put yourself in danger to rescue or treat an animal. Make sure the scene is safe before proceeding.

- Check the ABCs: airway, breathing, and circulation. Make sure the animal has an open airway, watch for breathing, and check for a pulse.

- Have a friend or neighbor that you can call to help you in case of an emergency. Have the phone numbers of your regular vet and the closest emergency veterinary hospital posted on your refrigerator. Know how to get to those hospitals so you won't panic when trying to find them for the first time. You can waste valuable time while trying to save your pet's life when you are driving around lost, and you may also be unable to drive safely.

- Attend a pet first aid course so you will learn how to take care of your pet in an emergency or if it just needs first aid treatment.

- Watch your pet to learn what is normal breathing for it. Learn where to check for its pulse.

- Learn how to medicate your pet. Ask veterinary technicians to show you their favorite tricks for giving pills to cats!

- Purchase or assemble a first aid kit. This will be especially helpful for dogs that hike or travel with their guardians.

- Make sure a pet carrier or collar and leash, or both, are always handy in case you have to transport your pet in a hurry. A securely closed pillowcase or laundry hamper can transport a small pet in an emergency.

Do not hesitate to call your veterinarian if you have any doubt about your pet's health. They are the best source of medical information.

How to Treat Abscesses

If your pet is acting fine, eating, and drinking, and the abscess has not burst, you can apply a warm compress. Warm compressing stimulates blood flow to the area and promotes drainage of the infected wound. Warm compressing also provides pain relief, but be prepared—this still may be painful, and you should use caution when doing this to your pet. Be careful not to use too warm of a compress, as the skin is already inflamed and very sensitive.

1. Wearing gloves, clip the fur, using clippers, around the area. This step may not be necessary, or your pet may not tolerate it.

2. Apply the compress to the area, using warm, moist, folded paper towels, gauze squares, or small washcloths. Very gently, press the warm, damp compress to the area. Repeat this several times daily to either encourage the abscess to begin to drain or to keep it open and draining as it is healing.

Always seek veterinary attention if your pet's condition worsens or if the abscess does not show improvement in a few days. Abscesses near the head, abdomen, and inside the legs should be examined by a veterinarian as soon as possible as these are places where healing may be difficult.

How to Stop Bleeding

A Bleeding Nail

If you are trimming your pet's nails for the first time or if your pet has dark nails, making it impossible to see where the quick is, you may cut the nail too short. When this happens, you may find yourself with a nail that won't stop bleeding. It may appear to be a large amount of blood, especially when your pet's blood pressure is up due to pain and excitement.

1. For minor cases, you can stop the bleeding by folding a paper towel and applying pressure until the bleeding stops.

2. If this doesn't stop the bleeding, you can use styptic powder, styptic sticks, or styptic pencil to promote the blood to clot. (You can purchase a styptic pencil at your pharmacy.) You can also use cornstarch, flour, or baking soda for this procedure. If you do not have any of these, you can use a sliver of very mild soap.

3. Pour the styptic powder, cornstarch, or flour into a small, shallow bowl. Wipe the blood off as well as you can, and dip the bleeding nail into the powder. If you are using a styptic stick, press the stick into the quick of the nail. The styptic powder and stick may cause stinging, so be prepared for your pet's reaction. If you are unable to place the dog's nail into the powder, add a little water to the powder to make a paste, and apply it with a cotton swab.

4. If the bleeding from the dog's nail is heavy, repeat the above steps.

5. If the bleeding is still not under control, following these steps, and—for additional protection from dirt and to prevent recurrence of bleeding—bandage the paw.

6. Place a folded paper towel or gauze squares over the bleeding nail. Wrap a length of roll gauze (securely but not tightly) around the paw to secure the folded towel or gauze squares. You can the put a sock over the paw or use self-adhering tape such as Coflex to create a clean and protective outer bandage. This should not need to stay on for more than a few hours. If bleeding continues, add another layer of gauze and tape.

7. Try to keep the pet quiet, and do not allow it to walk. Distract your pet, and do not let it lick the injured paw or the bandage.

8. Seek veterinary care as soon as possible if you are not able to control the bleeding.

Bleeding on Your Pet's Torso

1. Place a folded paper towel or gauze squares over the wound. Apply direct pressure for at least two minutes. Sanitary napkins work great for covering large wounds or wounds that are profusely bleeding.

2. Use roll gauze, torn sheets, etc., to secure the pad over the wound. If bleeding continues, do not remove the bloody bandage; add another layer of padding or gauze. You can also use self-adhering tape such as Coflex to create a clean and protective outer bandage.

3. Try to keep the pet quiet, and do not allow it to walk. Distract your pet, and do not let it lick or remove the bandage.

4. Seek veterinary care as soon as possible if you are not able to control the bleeding.

Bleeding From a Limb

Follow the above steps for bandaging. For severe bleeding, apply firm pressure using your fingers on the corresponding pressure point.

1. Front Leg: Use three fingers, and apply pressure to the area in the "armpit." This is the inside part of the upper front leg roughly between the shoulder and elbow.

2. Rear Leg: Use three fingers or the heel of your hand, and apply pressure in the groin area (inside of the thigh). This is where the

rear leg connects to the body. This is also the place where the pulse can be taken.

3. Tail: Use three fingers, and apply firm pressure on the underside of the tail base. You can also wrap your hand around the base of the tail with your thumb on the underside of the tail pressing in and your other fingers resting above the tail.

Elevating the limb reduces blood pressure by using gravity. This can slow bleeding. When combined with direct pressure, this is an effective way to stop bleeding.

Unless recommended by a veterinarian, do not use a tourniquet. Improperly placed, it can cause the loss of a limb.

Nosebleed

Possible causes of a nosebleed are traumatic injury, a foreign object, a nasal tumor, a bleeding disorder, or repeated sneezing.

1. Confine your pet, and try to keep it quiet.

2. Apply a cold compress to the nose. A frozen bag of peas wrapped on a small towel works great, as it conforms to the pet's face. Do not apply ice directly as it may cause tissue damage.

3. Do not tilt the head of an animal with a nosebleed back, as this may cause choking.

4. Do not pack the nostril with cotton balls, gauze, etc., as this may be irritating and cause more sneezing.

In any of the cases above, seek veterinary care as soon as possible if you are not able to control the bleeding.

Blood Sugar (Glucose) Problems

Diabetic pets may be at risk of developing high blood sugar (glucose), also called hyperglycemia. This is usually the result of uncontrolled diabetes. The symptoms of hyperglycemia can be similar to those of hypoglycemia. Left untreated, high blood sugar can cause health issues such as diabetic ketoacidosis (DKA). DKA is a serious medical emergency and can cause death if left untreated.

Signs of hyperglycemia include:

- confusion, disorientation, or staring into space

- fatigue, stumbling or staggering, weakness, depression

- shivering

- change in behavior

- vomiting

- increased drinking and urinating

You may also notice a characteristic smell to the breath described as fruity or smelling like nail polish remover. Not everyone has the ability to smell this, although it may be present. Seek veterinary care at once if you see any of the above signs and you suspect it may be high blood sugar.

Certain conditions may cause low blood sugar, also called hypogly-cemia. Hypoglycemia can occur when pets are on insulin or other medications to treat high blood sugar, have been exercised hard, if they are young animals and have been accidently kept from food, or have an illness or tumor as the cause. Hypoglycemia may occur with or without symptoms.

Signs of hypoglycemia include:

- ﹌ confusion, disorientation, or staring into space

- ﹌ fatigue, stumbling or staggering, weakness, depression

- ﹌ shivering

- ﹌ changes in behavior

- ﹌ Cats may make an odd vocalization.

If your pet is showing any of the above signs and you suspect it might be an issue with low blood sugar, give 1 to 2 teaspoons (5 to 10 ccs) liquid glucose, pancake syrup, corn syrup, or honey to your pet by mouth. Be very careful when administering this as your pet may be disoriented and may accidentally bite.

After giving the liquid, feed your pet its normal food or something your pet will reliably eat. (This may be from your arsenal of special foods.) While the syrup will give your pet a quick sugar boost, this boost will not last long. Your pet will need to eat a snack or meal to keep its blood sugar level up. Consult with your veterinarian to find the cause of this episode and to prevent it from reoccurring.

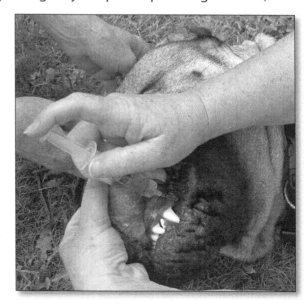

Do not put a volume of syrup into the mouth of an unconscious animal as it will not be able to

swallow it. Place one hand over the muzzle; lift up lip with thumb. Rub syrup onto the upper and lower gums. You can also put the syrup under the tongue.

If your pet does not respond quickly, call your veterinarian for instructions or take to the veterinary hospital immediately.

For more information on the care of diabetic pets, please refer to my book *Sugarbabies—A Holistic Guide to Caring for Your Diabetic Pet.*

CPR

Cardiopulmonary arrest is most simply defined as the abrupt, unexpected stopping of breathing and circulation. This may be the result of trauma or disease, as well as other causes.

Warning signs are changes in respiratory rate, depth, and pattern, a weak or irregular pulse, slow heart rate, low blood pressure, bluish gum color, and low body temperature.

Cardiopulmonary resuscitation provides artificial breathing, also called ventilation, and circulation to the patient.

What to do first: *Remember your ABCs!*

A: Establishment of an Airway. Check for any obstructions.

B: Breathing support. Start rescue breathing.

C: Circulation. Start CPR.

Unlike in human medicine, there are no specific guidelines for CPR for cats and dogs, although new protocols are being developed to help standardize this. Most information comes from veterinarians' clinical experience.

Before starting rescue breathing or CPR, check to make sure an animal is breathing. Next, check to see if the animal has a pulse.

How to Check if a Cat or Dog is Breathing

It may be difficult to tell if an animal is breathing if it has a thick hair coat or shallow breathing. An easy way to tell if an animal is breathing is to quickly pluck a few hairs from it and hold them up in front of one of its nostrils. If air is being expelled, you will see the hairs moving.

How to Check a Cat or Dog for a Heartbeat and Pulse

Method #1: With your pet laying on its right side, gently pull its front leg back and place your hand on its chest near the point of its elbow. You can often feel the heartbeat here, but you may not if it is a thick-coated animal or it has a weak heartbeat. Using a stethoscope is recommended.

Method #2: With your pet lying on its side, press your fingers gently inside either leg where the leg meets the body.

If the animal is not breathing but there is a pulse, start rescue breathing.

Rescue Breathing

Lay the animal on its right side, and elevate the body slightly higher than the head. Keep the head and neck straight to open the airway. Pull the tongue out to further open the airway. Cup your hands around the muzzle.

For a cat, blow into the nose/mouth for three seconds; wait two sec-onds and repeat. Repeat this sequence until the animal is breathing on its own or until you reach a veterinary hospital.

For a dog, blow into the nose/mouth for three seconds; repeat every three to five seconds until the animal is breathing on its own or until you reach a veterinary hospital.

If the animal is not breathing and there is no pulse, start CPR.

CPR can be done with one or two people. When done with one per-son, that person alternates breaths and compressions. When done with two people, one does the breathing while the other alternates with compressions. Note: When done with 2 people there is a slightly different ratio of breaths to compressions.

Cat:

Lay cat on its right side with its chest facing you. This can be done with one or two people.

One person: One breath per five chest compressions

Two people: One breath per three chest compressions

Dog:

Small dog (less than thirty pounds): Lay the dog on its right side with chest facing you.

One person: One breath per five chest compressions

Two people: One breath per three chest compressions

Large dog: Lay the dog on its right side with chest facing you.

One person: One breath per five chest compressions

Two people: One breath per three chest compressions

Giant Dog (more than ninety pounds): Lay the dog on its right side with chest away from you.

One person: One breath per ten chest compressions

Two people: One breath per six chest compressions

❧ Do CPR at the widest part of the chest.

❧ After two minutes, stop and check for a pulse and breathing.

❧ Do CPR for a maximum of twenty minutes.

Use of Acupuncture to Stimulate Respiration

There is an acupuncture point that is located toward the top of the division between an animal's nose and lip, also called the nasal philtrum. (See photo.) In acupuncture terms, this is GV 26—the twenty-sixth point on the Governing Vessel meridian. Stimulating this point helps the body to release adrenaline. Adrenaline is the natural version of the drug epinephrine, a drug used in human and veterinary medicine to stimulate the heartbeat and breathing.

If an animal is not breathing, insert a pen cap, safety pin, paper-clip, fingernail, small-gauge needle, etc., and twirl it vigorously or move it up and down in a pecking motion while watching for respiration. Repeat for at least twenty minutes or until you see the animal begin to breathe on its own or you reach the veterinary hospital. Do not worry if you see a drop of blood; this is normal.

The author has successfully used this technique on newborn kittens and puppies born by cesarean section as well as with animals under anesthesia.

GV26 acupuncture point —> •

Alternative CPR Technique

Interposed Abdominal Compression (IAC-CPR) is an alternative CPR technique. This method can be done by pressing down on the abdomen, closest to the head, between each chest compression. It is thought to be very effective in forcing blood to the heart and brain.

Checking Gum Color and Capillary Refill Time (CRT)

The gums are actually mucous membranes and are a good indicator of blood circulation and how well oxygenated the blood is. Normal gum color is pink. It may be difficult to tell the gum color on pets with pigmented (dark) gums. By gently lowering the eyelid, you can more easily tell the mucous membrane color on these pets. Contact your veterinarian immediately if your pet's gums are pale, white, blue, or yellow.

Capillary refill time is a crude method of checking circulation. Normal refill time is one to two seconds. Refill times of less than one second or over three seconds indicate a problem that needs immediate veterinary intervention.

1. Make sure your pet is comfortable with you putting your fingers in its mouth. It is not worth getting bitten to perform this test.

2. Using a fingertip, quickly apply pressure to the gums, and release. The area should turn white then rapidly turn back to the normal pink color.

3. Count the number of seconds the return to pink takes.

Chocolate Toxicity

Chocolate toxicity is something that can affect a pet any time of year, but it seems to happen more commonly around holiday time when chocolate is more readily available. The active ingredient in chocolate is *theobromine*.

The concentration of theobromine varies with the formulation of the chocolate.

- Milk chocolate has forty-four milligrams per ounce. A toxic dose for a fifty-pound dog is fifty ounces.

- Semisweet chocolate has one hundred fifty milligrams per ounce. A toxic dose for a fifty-pound dog is fifteen ounces.

- Baking chocolate has three hundred ninety milligrams per ounce. A toxic dose for a fifty pound dog is five ounces.

The signs of chocolate toxicity include nervousness, vomiting, diarrhea, muscle tremors, seizures, coma, and death.

If you suspect that your pet has ingested chocolate, call your veterinarian or animal emergency clinic at once and follow their directions.

You may be told that you just need to watch your pet for any signs, that you need to induce vomiting (see below), or that you need to get medical care for your pet at once.

Cold-Related Emergencies

Hypothermia is a low core body temperature. Hypothermia is especially dangerous if the animal is young, elderly, or in poor health. Be especially careful after bathing pets and with pets that spend time outdoors in wet weather. Drying a cold, wet animal will help lessen heat loss.

The signs of hypothermia are shivering, stumbling or lack of coordination, body temperature below 95°F (35°C), slow respiration rate, and slow pulse rate.

What to do:

1. Remove the animal from the cold environment, and enclose it in a small space such as a dog kennel or warm bathroom.

2. Provide heat such as a warm, thick blanket, warm towels from the dryer, space blanket, heat disc, warm pet bed, or heat vent. You may also give a warm bath, provided you can thoroughly dry the pet with a blow-dryer afterward.

3. Take the pet's rectal temperature every ten to fifteen minutes until it reaches 101°F (38.3°C).

The signs of severe hypothermia are a core body temperature below 90°F (32.2°C), shivering that has stopped, stiff and rigid muscles, very slow pulse and respiration, and an animal that may appear dead.

What to do:

1. Remove the animal from the cold environment, and enclose it in a small space such as a warm bathroom.

2. Be careful moving the pet. Use support; avoid twisting or moving it too much. Treat the animal as very fragile.

3. Cover the pet to keep it warm with a blanket, warm towels, etc.

4. Do not try vigorously to warm the animal up; you may cause more harm.

5. *Seek veterinary care immediately.*

Heat-Related Emergencies

Heat-related emergencies can occur when pets are left in very hot cars, when they exercise too strenuously in hot, humid weather, and when they suffer from medical conditions such as laryngeal paralysis or circulatory conditions. Short-nosed dogs such as Pugs, Bulldogs, and Boxers are more commonly affected. Cat breeds such as Persians may also be more susceptible.

Signs:

᠗ Rapid panting

᠗ Elevated heart rate

᠗ Red gums

᠗ Decreased level of consciousness

᠗ In most cases, elevated body temperature above 103°F

᠗ Vomiting/diarrhea

᠗ Seizures

᠗ Bruising

What to do:

1. Move the animal to a cool, well-ventilated area.

2. Soak coat with *cool* water. (Do not use cold water as it may cause a dangerously low body temperature.)

3. Apply cool packs to groin, armpits, and neck, or you can lay a pet on a cool, damp towel.

4. Transport the animal to the veterinarian for evaluation.

Diarrhea

There are many causes of diarrhea. Sometimes it is a normal reaction as the body tries to expel something that is making it ill. Diarrhea can also be the result of a virus, overgrowth of bacteria, eating spoiled food, eating food an animal is allergic to, disease, or parasites. Cases of simple diarrhea may pass uneventfully, while more prolonged cases can result in weakness, dehydration, or even death in very compromised animals.

Children's electrolyte solution can be added to food or water, but never replace a pet's water with this. Another product that can be used is Virbac's Rebound OES (oral electrolyte solution). This is a chicken flavored ready-to-use formula that contains electrolytes to help replace fluids in dogs and cats.

Feeding a bland diet can help in cases where the pet has over eaten or has eaten something that has not agreed with their system. You will find more information on bland diets in the section below on Vomiting.

Over the counter kaolin/pectin preparations made specifically for pets can be very effective for simple cases of diarrhea.

If your pet suffers from chronic diarrhea or diarrhea that is worsening or uncontrolled for more than a day or two, consult with your veterinarian. If diarrhea is accompanied by vomiting or if your pet is acting unwell, seek veterinary attention at once.

Seizures

Witnessing a cat or dog having a seizure can be frightening. Even if you have seen seizures before, it can be a very distressing sight.

There are some key points to remember when a pet is having a seizure:

- Remain calm. This is easier said than done, but it is very important. Try to time how long the seizure lasts.

- Do not try to comfort the animal, as this is a time when many people are accidentally bitten. The animal is in a state of mind where it does not recognize you. Please remember, an animal cannot swallow its tongue.

- Take away anything your pet may harm itself on and, if you are able to do it safely, quickly throw something down to cushion its head if it is lying on a hard surface.

- Remove any further stimulus from your pet by doing the following:

  - Ask any unnecessary people to leave the area. Remove any other pets that may be disturbed by the seizure. Animals can react in several ways to a seizing animal, and sometimes they may be disturbed enough to attack.

  - Turn off any loud music or TV.

  - Dim the lights.

In very warm or hot weather, once the animal has recovered, safely allow it to get some fresh air or take it to a cool or well-ventilated place.

Call your veterinarian or emergency hospital for further instructions.

Seizures become an emergency, requiring immediate veterinary attention, when the following happens. A continual seizure is called *status epilepticus*. Medical intervention is needed to stop the seizure. Without intervention, brain and organ damage can result from increased body temperature (hyperthermia), metabolic imbalance (acidosis), reduced blood flow (hypoperfusion), and reduced oxygen to tissues (hypoxia). These functions also occur with a smaller seizure, and this is why any pet suffering from seizures on a regular basis needs to have them brought under control.

The Three Phases of Seizures

1. Preictal. This is the "before" stage of a seizure. Sometimes you may not notice these signs. Right before a seizure, some animals get very still, act disoriented or dazed, or become restless and vocalize. This stage can last for a few seconds or minutes.

2. Ictus is the seizure itself. Animals may fall over on their sides, whimper, urinate, defecate, drool, and do vigorous paddling with their limbs. This stage may last a few seconds or minutes.

3. Postictal phase is the "after" time of the seizure. Some animals will be sleepy, while other animals act as if nothing happened. Some animals appear dazed, disoriented, or confused. Some will pant heavily or breathe with their mouths open. They may also appear blind or unable to walk well and will bump into things. Often, animals act very hungry and will go right over to their bowls to eat. This period can last from several minutes to several hours.

If your pet is prone to seizures, restricting it from certain situations may help prevent recurrence of seizures. Avoid loud noises, such as fireworks, as well as visual stimulation from TV or video games.

TPR - Temperature, Pulse, and Respiration

Taking a TPR is a standard way of monitoring pets in the hospital, and you can also do it at home. Taking your pet's TPR can give you and your veterinarian a wealth of information about your pet's current health.

Temperature: Taking a rectal temperature is more reliable than using an ear thermometer. Just because an animal has a warm nose does not mean it is running a fever. Animals have higher body temperatures and should feel warmer than we do. But you can often feel that the ears of an animal with a fever are especially warm. Taking the temperature is the only true way of knowing if your pet is running a fever.

Cats may have elevated temperatures due to stress in the veterinary office or from being in a cat carrier in a warm car on the way to the vet visit.

After exercising or eating a meal, your pet's temperature may be slightly higher.

A dog's normal body temperature should be between 100.5°F (38.0° C) and 102.5°F (39.2° C)

A cat's normal body temperature should be between 100.5°F (38.0° C) and 102.5°F (39.2° C)

How to take your pet's temperature:

1. Enlist help to restrain your pet. (See Chapter 10.) With the animal facing away from you, gently lift the tail. Be especially gentle

with elderly animals that may have sore hips, back problems, or arthritis.

2. Lubricate the thermometer.

3. Insert the thermometer an inch or two into the pet's rectum.

4. Listen for the beep of the digital thermometer, or wait for two minutes if you are using a mercury thermometer (not recommended).

5. Remove the thermometer from your pet, and check the reading.

6. Clean the thermometer with alcohol so it will be ready for its next use.

Contact your veterinarian if your pet's temperature is below 99°F (37.2° C) or above 103°F (39.4° C).

To cool down an animal with a fever, you can place cool, damp cloths on its head, on its groin area, and under its front legs close to its chest. You can also put rubbing alcohol on the foot pads of an animal to help lower its temperature when it has a very high fever, although this may not be very effective. *Do not give your pet any medications for reducing fever in people—they can be toxic!*

Heart rate or pulse: The pulse is a transmitted heartbeat, and you can feel it with your fingers. You should be able to feel the pulse at the same time as each heartbeat. Do not use your thumb when feeling for a pulse; use your ring, index, or middle finger. Using your thumb may result in you mistaking your own pulse for your pet's.

The easiest place to find your pet's pulse is in the crease where the back legs and groin join together. This is where the femoral artery is located. There are other pulse points in the front legs and neck area, but they are not as easy to feel.

1. Make sure you have a watch or clock with a second hand readily available.

2. When your pet is lying on its side, press your fingers in the area of the femoral artery until you feel the pulse. You may have to have someone gently distract your pet while you are doing this, although most animals will not mind the intrusion.

3. Count the pulses you feel in fifteen seconds, and multiply by four. This is the beats per minute (BPM). You can also count for ten seconds and multiply by six.

Larger dogs have slower rates than small dogs, and athletic dogs have lower heart rates than dogs of similar age and size that are not physically fit.

Puppies and kittens usually have higher heart rates than adults— around two hundred beats per minute.

When stressed, even a healthy animal's heart rate will increase, but it will normalize as the animal relaxes. Cats with heart conditions such as cardiomyopathy or diseases such as hyperthyroidism will have increased heart rates, often more than two hundred or three hundred beats per minute. In these cases, a cat's heart rate will still be very high even when resting at home.

A dog's normal beats per minute is sixty to one hundred for large breeds, and one hundred to one hundred forty for small breeds.

A cat's normal beats per minute is one hundred twenty to one hundred forty, although it may be normal for some cats to have a heart rate up to one hundred eighty beats per minute.

Respiratory rate: Respiratory rate is the number of breaths per minute when an animal is resting. Animals that are in pain, have heart or respiratory disease, or are overheated or excited have higher respiratory rates.

For dogs, ten to thirty-five breaths per minute is normal, unless panting.

For cats, fifteen to forty breaths per minute is normal. It is not normal for a cat to pant unless it is frightened. Open-mouth breathing is not normal for cats.

Normally, a pet's chest expands as the air enters the lungs. The chest then contracts as the breath leaves the lungs. This should be an even and smooth movement that does not require much effort. What is not normal is breathing that looks like it is coming from the abdominal area, gasping, open-mouth breathing, noisy breathing, shallow breathing, or excessive panting. Consult your veterinarian immediately if you notice any of these signs.

Wound Care

If you notice a fresh wound on your pet and it is bleeding, the first step is to put direct pressure on it to stop the bleeding. A wound that is contaminated with dirt, gravel, glass, etc., needs to be flushed clean. It can be flushed, or irrigated, using warm water in a syringe. Specialized, curved-tip syringes are available for wound irrigation. Remember, this may sting, so be prepared for your pet's reaction.

Ask your veterinarian for a suggestion for what to have in your first aid kit for cleaning simple wounds. He or she may recommend or dispense a diluted solution of chlorhexidine, betadine, surgical scrub soap, or something else.

A wound heals best when it is slightly moist. The skin around it should be kept clean and dry.

For cleaning simple wounds, you can also make your own saline solution by mixing one teaspoon of Epsom salts or table salt in two cups of warm water.

Do not use:

- Hydrogen peroxide

- Alcohol

- Shampoo

- Soap

- Solutions made with essential oils or tea tree oil

Even diluted hydrogen peroxide can damage the skin and delay wound healing. The reason your fingers turn white when you handle hydrogen peroxide is because it is damaging the skin cells. Please see Chapter 15 for more information on bandage care.

Vomiting

Vomiting is a very common problem in dogs and cats. Vomiting is also known as emesis and is the forceful expulsion of the stomach contents through the mouth. Usually partially digested food is present in vomit, and it may be mixed with fluid. If the fluid is yellow, bile may be present. There are many causes of vomiting, including:

- Eating garbage or spoiled food

- Internal parasites

- Food allergies

- A foreign body in the stomach or intestine

- Gastritis (inflammation of stomach lining)

- Hair balls that form when large amounts of hair are ingested during grooming

- Hyperthyroidism, in cats

- Stomach ulcers

- Kidney and liver disease

- Stomach or upper intestinal cancer

- Balance disorders

- Ingesting toxins such as insecticides, antifreeze, and other chemicals

- Bacterial and viral infections

Vomiting can be confused with regurgitation. Regurgitation is the passive ejection of contents of the esophagus, a narrow, muscular tube. Food passes through the esophagus on its way to the stomach. When an animal regurgitates, the food brought up is usually undigested and may have a tubular shape. Regurgitation often happens right after eating, especially if the pet has eaten quickly.

If the vomit contains blood, it may be fresh, red blood, also called frank blood. Digested blood in the vomit will resemble coffee grounds. Even pets with empty stomachs may try to vomit.

For mild cases of acute (sudden) vomiting:

1. Withhold food and water for twelve to twenty-four hours to give the pet's digestive system a chance to rest. Do not withhold water from an animal with diagnosed or possible kidney disease. Do not withhold food from a diabetic pet and continue to give insulin injections. If you live in a very hot or dry climate or your pet has other medical concerns discuss with your

veterinarian the length of time you should be withholding food and water.

2. If there is no more vomiting, feed small amounts of a bland low-fat food three to six times daily for a few days. Also reintroduce small amounts of water. Do not allow your pet to consume large amounts of water at one time.

3. If the pet continues to tolerate the bland diet, gradually increase the amount you feed and gradually transition back to the pet's normal diet.

A bland diet can include cooked barley, which is excellent to use, rice, or potatoes, along with small portions of cooked skinless chicken. Cooked ground beef or turkey can also be used but must be very thoroughly drained of as much fat as possible.

An animal that vomits for more than one to two days or is showing other signs of illness, including fever, lethargy, diarrhea, depression, and dehydration, should be examined by a veterinarian as soon as possible.

When and How to Induce Vomiting

There may be times when it is beneficial to induce your dog or cat to vomit. *If possible, consult your veterinarian, emergency clinic, or veterinary poison hotline before you attempt this.* It will be very helpful if you can tell them exactly what your pet has ingested, how much was ingested, and what the ingredients of the substance are, especially the active ingredients.

Do not induce vomiting when:

1. Your pet has already vomited.

2. You know or suspect your pet has ingested a household cleaning product, petroleum product, or a product containing acids or alkalis. These chemicals may cause more damage when vomited.

3. You know or suspect your pet has swallowed a sharp object.

4. It is possible the poison was ingested more than two hours before.

5. The package of what your pet has ingested says "Do Not Induce Vomiting."

6. You are not sure what kind or how much poison your pet has ingested.

7. Your pet is having seizures, is unconscious, or is having trouble breathing.

Cats: The most reliable and safe way to induce vomiting in a cat is to use hydrogen peroxide. Do not use dry mustard or syrup of ipecac. Never use expired syrup of ipecac as it can be deadly. The correct dose is 0.5 ml of hydrogen peroxide per pound.

1. Weigh your pet.

2. Use only a *3 percent solution* of hydrogen peroxide. Determine your dose by multiplying your cat's weight by 0.5. For example, a ten-pound cat would get 5 ml of hydrogen peroxide. (Five mls = 1 teaspoon.)

3. Draw the hydrogen peroxide into a clean syringe and give as you would oral liquid medication. (See Chapter 9 for how to give liquids by mouth.)

4. After giving the dose, encourage your cat to walk around. Getting your cat moving and patting its abdomen helps to mix the hydrogen peroxide with the stomach contents. Vomiting should occur within twenty minutes. If it does not, seek veterinary advice if possible. Repeating the dose just once may be necessary.

Dogs: Follow the same dose and instructions as for cats. You can measure out and give the hydrogen peroxide with a turkey baster if you do not have a large enough syringe.

Do not leave your pet unattended while trying to induce vomiting. Dogs will often immediately eat what they have just vomited, so be prepared to get your pet away from it quickly.

If you are successful at getting your pet to vomit, collect a sample of the vomit, the packaging from the substance, and, if possible, a sample of what was ingested. Take these to your veterinarian so he or she can try to evaluate what poison was eaten and treat accordingly.

Pet First Aid Kits

First aid kits for pets can be purchased in stores or online. You can also assemble them with items from the following list. Keep all items in a waterproof plastic bin.

- One-inch medical or bandage tape

- Alcohol or antibacterial wipes

- Antibacterial soap and shampoo

- Antibiotic ointment. If you can find double antibiotic ointment, get that instead. Some animals (just like people) can have reactions to neomycin, a component of triple antibiotic ointment.

- Bandage scissors

- Bulb syringe (for suctioning mucus from nostrils of newborn or congested pets)

- Cornstarch or styptic to stop nail bleeding

- Cotton swabs

- Different sizes of syringes (do not need to be sterile if used for oral medication)

- Digital thermometer (a pediatric thermometer is great for cats, kittens, and small dogs)

- Disposable plastic gloves

- Eyewash

- First aid guide

- Hydrogen peroxide, 3 percent

- Ice and heat packs

- Instant hand sanitizer

- Large irrigation syringe (or turkey baster)

- Leash

- Magnifying glass

- Muzzle

- Penlight with fresh batteries

- Pet CPR barrier. This is a piece of plastic wrap with a hole in that makes an effective barrier between you and your patient when you are doing rescue breathing

- Rescue Remedy liquid or cream or Five Flower Formula liquid

- Saline solution in a squirt bottle

- Small and large towel or blanket

- Space blanket

- Sterile gauze pads and gauze roll

- Stethoscope (can be purchased from nursing or medical supply stores)

- Stiff cardboard or small wooden splint (use cardboard rolls from toilet tissue and paper towels)

- Cohesive bandage material such as Vet Wrap

- Tongue depressors

- Triangular bandage (to make a muzzle or sling)

- Tweezers

- The name, address, telephone number, and hours of your veterinarian and the nearest emergency veterinary clinic. Include directions if needed.

⚜

CHAPTER 17
When to Call Your Veterinarian

What you will learn in this chapter:

ﾟﾟ What the signs that your pet needs to see a veterinarian are

ﾟﾟ What the signs of a possibly life-threatening situation are

ﾟﾟ What basic information you should know about your veterinarian

There are times when a little bit of nursing care and TLC will get your pet through a day or two of feeling under the weather. At other times, it is important to seek professional medical care as soon as possible. While it is very easy to look up information on the Internet, please remember, there is no substitute for a physical exam and advice given by a trained veterinarian.

In many communities, there are twenty-four-hour clinics that can give free opinions on the phone on whether something needs to be seen. Most day practices can also do this. Keep in mind, it may be difficult for them to give you a definite answer, so if you have any doubt, please make an appointment for your pet to be examined.

Note: Items in bold designate a possible life-threatening situation. Seek medical care immediately!

Seek veterinary care for your pet ASAP when you notice the following:

- **Your pet is disoriented, lethargic, or uncoordinated**

- **Your pet is walking unsteadily or appears weak**

- **Your pet is having continual seizures**

- **Your pet's abdomen appears bloated**

- **Your pet is hyperactive or especially restless and nervous**

- **Your pet's temperature is above 103°F (37.2°C) or below 99°F (39.4°C)**

- Your pet is reluctant to get up or to move

- Your pet is limping for more than 2 days

- Your pet cries out when touched or when moving

- Your pet is walking in circles or has a head tilt

- Your pet appears dehydrated

- **Your pet is open-mouth breathing**

- **Your pet is breathing with extra effort or its breathing is irregular, very rapid, or shallow**

- **Your pet has facial swelling**

- **Your pet has very red, bluish, brownish, or very pale gums**

- **Your pet is salivating profusely**

- **Your pet's breath smells like acetone or nail polish remover (ketones)**

- **Your pet has trouble swallowing or is constantly gulping**

- Your pet has blood, mucus, or pus coming from its nose

- Your pet's nose is blocked, and it cannot breath out of it

- You can hear crackling sounds in your pet's chest when it breathes

- Your pet has inflamed or bleeding gums

- Your pet's breath has a very foul smell

- Your pet is unwilling to eat for more than a day or two

- Your pet is or unable to eat although it appears interested in food

- Your pet has severe diarrhea (without other signs of illness) for more than 1 day or it contains blood

- Your pet is vomiting (without other signs of illness) more than 2 days or 5-6 times in one day

- (Note: Vomiting and diarrhea can be simple or very complicated conditions-please seek veterinary advice at once when they are in addition to other signs of illness.)

- Your pet is constipated for more than 1-2 days

- **Your male cat or dog is repeatedly attempting to urinate and not producing any urine**

- Your pet has swelling, inflammation, or sores in its anal area

- Your pet is straining to urinate or urinating in unusual places

- Your pet is constantly licking under its tail

- Your pet has blood in its urine

- Your pet is losing hair

- Your pet is constantly scratching

- Your pet has irritated skin with sores and scabs

- Your pet's skin has a bad smell

- Your pet has lumps and bumps on its skin

- **Your pet's pupils are unevenly dilated**

- **Your pet's eyes are overly dilated**

- Your pet has cloudy, watery, or irritated eyes

- Your pet's eyes have discolored discharge

- Your pet is squinting

- Your pet is constantly pawing at or rubbing its eyes

- You can see your pet's third eyelid

- Your pet seems very sensitive to light

- Your pet's ears have waxy, discolored, or black discharge

- You pet's ears have a foul or yeasty smell

- Your pet's ears are red and inflamed

- Your pet is constantly shaking its head

- Your pet is constantly scratching or rubbing its ears

- Your pet will not let you touch or examine its ears

- Your pet has sores, scabs, or hair loss on its ears

Make sure that you know your veterinarian's phone number, payment policies, and days and hours of operation. If your veterinarian does not provide after-hours service, is there an emergency hospital in your area? Make sure you have that information also, as well as clear directions to find the facility. If you are driving around lost, you may delay your pet from receiving lifesaving treatment.

CHAPTER 18

Taking Good Care of Your Senior Pet

What you will learn in this chapter:

- What physical and emotional changes your pet may be experiencing

- What you can do to make your pet more comfortable

- What you can do to keep your pet safe

- What Cognitive Dysfunction Syndrome (CDS) is

- How to spot trouble and when to take your pet to the veterinarian

Physical changes occur in an animal's body as it ages. Around midlife (which varies widely in cats and dogs), an animal's internal systems will begin to slow down. In dogs, midlife may start anywhere from four to eight years; in cats, it may start at seven years and up. Physical changes may not be very noticeable in some pets. This is why, as an animal ages, veterinary visits and periodic blood work are very important. Taking good care of your senior pet starts with understanding some of the changes your pet may be experiencing.

Changes that Accompany Aging

Metabolic rate slows down. This, combined with the fact that calories consumed often exceed the energy used in the body, results in weight gain. Studies have shown that weight gain is a contributing factor in the onset of diabetes in some animals. This extra weight can also cause painful joints and can make normal movement more difficult. It is very important to feed a high-quality food that contains the appropriate ingredients and meets the calorie requirements for your pet. A *consistent* and *daily* exercise program can also help greatly to regulate weight and maintain overall good health.

Hormone production is decreased. Imbalances in hormones can result in such diseases as hyperthyroidism (mainly in cats), hypothyroidism (mainly in dogs), and diabetes mellitus. Blood tests are recommended to diagnose these diseases.

Regulation of body temperature is impaired. Aging pets face difficulty in regulating body temperature in part because their blood vessels become less able to contract and dilate in response to cold and heat. As an animal's ability to regulate its own body temperature greatly diminishes, cold weather can be very difficult for older animals to tolerate. It is not recommended that pets be left outside, but if you must, you should take special precautions. Providing cozy sleeping places inside will also be greatly appreciated. Many animals benefit from a heated bed; this can also help with aching joints. Another simple thing your pet may enjoy is having you warm a small blanket or towel in the dryer and laying it over your pet when it is lying down. Its coziness may help your pet relax and may also help relieve achiness.

Many pets will also become less tolerant of heat. It is especially important to make sure they do not get overheated and that in warm weather they have fresh, smoke-free, and well-ventilated air.

Circulation diminishes. Some of the problems associated with diminished circulation include cold paws and extremities, slow wound healing, dry skin, fur loss, and fatigue. An elderly pet's heart may be less efficient at pumping blood. The results of this include less oxygen-rich blood reaching the brain and tissues. Less oxygen reaching the lungs can cause exercise intolerance and fatigue. This is another reason providing your pet with fresh, smoke-free, and well-ventilated air is vital for its good health.

As a result of the aging process, the skin becomes less elastic and more easily damaged. Please see Chapter 11 for more information.

An elderly pet's digestive system is less efficient at processing food; therefore, it is more difficult for its body to use nutrients. In addition, smell and taste are duller in an older pet, which can result in a poor appetite. In the older pet, there are fewer taste buds, and the sense of smell may decline. This may cause a lack of appetite. There may be times when you need to tempt your pet with warmed foods and find healthy treats to stimulate appetite. Use caution with the amount of treats you feed your pet. (See Chapter 6 for more information on nutrition.)

The digestive system may encounter changes, and feeding smaller meals may be easier on your pet's system. Keep in mind there are different philosophies on how best to feed your pet. By doing your own research and with your veterinarian's help, you can determine which method is best for feeding your pet. Again, consistency is key, and you may be advised to feed your pet the way it is used to.

Often, older pets benefit from food and water bowls that are elevated. If they have arthritis or stiffness in their necks, eating from an elevated bowl will be make eating more comfortable for them. It may also help the older pet that is having problems with its esophagus.

Constipation may also be a problem in the older pet. This may be a cause for an animal to lose its appetite or even vomit. Talk to your veterinarian if you think your pet appears to be constipated, even occasionally, as the problem is much easier to treat if noticed early and prevented before it becomes severe. If several people are walking the dog or cleaning the cat's litter box, devise a system so that you know exactly what your pet's fecal output is.

The longer stool stays in a pet's body, the harder and drier it becomes. This can lead to constipation as well as a pet "holding it" because it is painful to defecate. Give your pet every opportunity to pass stool when it needs to. For cats, this means having one or more litter boxes in very convenient places. Your elderly cat may be "holding it" because it doesn't want to make the trip to the cold, dark garage where the litter box is kept or has difficulty getting up or down the steps to reach it. For dogs, make sure they have plenty of opportunities and time to "do their business" outside. Use patience with the frequency and time it may take them as they age. Dehydration can be a cause of constipation. Because of this and other reasons, it is vitally important that your pet stays well hydrated. See Chapter 8 for more information.

Make sure that your pet is not "mechanically constipated". This is the term used when a pet has long hair or mats under its tail preventing it from having a bowel movement.

Dental problems, which are often present, can make eating difficult for older pets. Tartar may build up on the teeth and push the gums back, allowing bacteria to more easily infect the gums. Large amounts of dental bacteria floating around in the bloodstream can have serious consequences on the health of the heart and kidneys. Talk to your veterinarian about what kind of dental work your pet may need. It may be a simple dental cleaning or may involve tooth removal. There may be additional costs for dental work for seniors, since your pet should have IV fluids and may require extra monitoring while under anesthesia.

Many dental problems can be evaluated at the time of your pet's physical exam. There are also signs you can watch for at home that alert you to any problems.

An animal with a painful mouth may exhibit some or all of the following behaviors:

- Reluctance to eat although it shows interest in food

- Chewing on only one side of its mouth

- Food falling from its mouth while eating

- Pawing at the side of its mouth

- Taking only one or two bites of food, then walking away

- Weight loss

- Facial swelling

- Foul-smelling breath

An animal with an infected tooth may show a swelling on the face as well as have very foul-smelling breath. Any of the above signs are reasons to take your pet in for an exam with your vet.

Eyesight becomes less acute as thickening of the lenses occurs, and occasionally cataracts may appear. Diminishing eyesight can be very serious for animals left on their own outside. For the indoor cat, this may be a reason the kitty is not making it to the litter box in the middle of the night. It is a good idea to provide lighting in places pets frequent at night, as well as safeguard animals with impaired eyesight from steps, balconies, and other places from which they could fall.

Cataracts are common in diabetic dogs, but not in cats. Cataract formation may happen quickly in dogs, in a matter of days, or it may take years. Once formed, cataracts are irreversible, but they can be surgically removed by a veterinary ophthalmologist. There is generally a high success rate in restoring vision with this procedure, although there are several factors that determine success. These factors include how well regulated the diabetic dog's blood sugar is, as well as the general health of the eye. A veterinary ophthalmologist can discuss your dog's medical status with you to determine if your pet would be a good surgical candidate.

Other eye problems noted in the senior pet include ulcerations, inflammations, slow-healing wounds, and lesions. This is another reason why periodic exams are very important.

Hearing becomes less acute, and internal changes may make the hearing less sensitive. Wax may also build up, dulling sounds that can get through. Your veterinarian can examine your pet's ears with an otoscope to make sure there is not a medical problem (infection, ear mites, wax, and growths) that may be the reason for hearing loss.

Be careful to not startle a sleeping pet that may not hear you. Be very careful with outdoor pets when starting up and moving cars. Also be aware that your pet may not hear you calling it, and you will need extra patience and perhaps another system besides your voice for keeping your pet close to you on walks or when out in the backyard.

Muscle tone and volume diminishes, making the animal move more slowly and with less agility. Both dogs and cats can suffer from arthritis. Provide ramps, stairs, or step stools so those pets will have an easier time getting on the couch or bed or in the car. Use rubber-backed rugs or mats throughout the house to give your pet a nonslip surface on smooth flooring. There are a number of nutritional supplements and medications to help arthritic animals with their pain. *Never use human pain medication without discussing it with your veterinarian first.* Cats in particular can be poisoned by some human pain medications.

Cut down the sides of the litter box to make it easier for elderly cats to step into. An under-the-bed sweater box makes a great low-sided and large litter box, perfect for elderly cats. Keep the cat litter to only about one-and-a-half to two inches to make it easier for your cat to get its footing inside the box.

The urinary system may experience some changes. It is important to pay special attention to signs such as:

- Urinating (or trying to urinate) frequently and in unusual places

- Cats that constantly go in and out of the litter box

- If your male cat or dog are straining and producing no urine, *seek immediate medical care, as this may be life-threatening.* Female animals can also strain and not produce urine, but not due to a life-threatening urinary obstruction as in the male animal.

- Blood in the urine

- Strong-smelling urine

- Vocalizing when urinating

- Frequently licking under the tail

Report any of these signs to your veterinarian at once. Not only are urinary infections unhealthy, but they are also very uncomfortable for your pet. It is also important to pay close attention to litter box hygiene and watch for signals that your dog needs to go out to urinate. Some people think their pets may no longer be housebroken, when it may simply be that they cannot get to the appropriate place to urinate quickly enough.

Middle-aged and older spayed dogs may also be prone to incontinence when sleeping or relaxing. Some may merely dribble urine, while others pass a large amount of urine while being unaware. Discuss this with your veterinarian, as there are medications than can help with this problem.

Cognitive Dysfunction Syndrome

Mental function can decline in senior cats and dogs. This is often called Cognitive Dysfunction Syndrome (CDS) and is similar to Alzheimer's disease in humans. CDS can cause a wide range of behavioral changes. Generally, the changes occur in the pet's activity level, sleep patterns, appetite, and social interactions. Many pets may appear disoriented, have lost their house-training habits, play or exercise less, vocalize in a distant part of the house as if lost, fail to recognize family, wander aimlessly, and stare into space. Some pets may become aggressive with other animals, fearful, or anxious.

Currently there are no diagnostic tests for CDS, but veterinarians evaluate observations reported by guardians and try to rule out other possible causes for the changes. After a diagnosis of CDS has been reached, education is the first step in treatment as many people become frustrated with their pet's changing behavior. The pet is not being naughty or lazy, and they need extra patience at this point in their lives. Your veterinarian can discuss the use of medications and diet to help with the changes. Thoughtful consideration as to what may make the pet's life easier can also help in many ways.

If you suspect your pet may have CDS:

- Schedule a physical exam with your veterinarian

- Limit your pet's stress and exposure to stressful situations

- Keep your pet mentally stimulated

- Reinforce basic commands and be more vigilant with house-training

- Supervise your pet with other pets if problems occur

- Be patient!

Keeping Your Pet Safe

Keep your elderly pet safe and out of harm's way. Many animals may wander or become lost. Make sure they stay safely contained and away from steps or dangerous places. *Make sure your pet has*

ID on it at all times or is microchipped, or both. A microchip is a small device that is implanted under your pet's skin in the area between the shoulder blades. Your pet's microchip will contain a number that is registered to you. In the event that your pet becomes lost and is found, the finder can have your pet scanned at a veterinary clinic, shelter, or some police stations. Every day in the news are stories of people reunited with pets thanks to a microchip. Remember, it is your responsibility to keep your registered contact information current. Some people choose to have a tag that alerts people to a specific medical condition such as diabetes should someone else find the pet. This is an excellent way to ensure that your pet receives the treatment it needs while awaiting its return to you. Containment systems like the Purr-fect Cat Fence are an excellent way for pets to continue to enjoy the great outdoors safely.

Many behavioral problems may be medical in origin. At any point in your pet's life, especially when being treated for an illness or chronic condition, your pet should have a full physical exam and blood work run to rule out a medical condition that may be a cause for behavior issues. It is recommended to do this every six months, as problems in older pets may arise or worsen suddenly. Many undesirable behaviors from pets are caused by medical problems and by being in pain or discomfort. Addressing and treating those needs are very important for keeping your older pet happy and comfortable.

In conclusion, many changes take place in the bodies and minds of our older pets. As guardians of our beloved furry friends, we can continue to enjoy their company well into their golden years. With good veterinary care, optimal nutrition, and attention to our pets' emotional needs, senior pets can live long and comfortable lives. Advanced age is not a reason for euthanasia!

∾✺∿

CHAPTER 19

Hospice Care

_____

What you will learn in this chapter:

∾ What the basic concepts in hospice care are

∾ How to know if hospice care is right for your pet

∾ What questions you should ask yourself when deciding to put your pet in hospice care

Basics of Hospice Care

Some people choose to discontinue medical treatment and allow their pets to pass away naturally in a hospice setting at home. But this doesn't mean that treatments have to end. Many treatments can be provided in the home setting, such as physical therapy, massage therapy, pain management, acupuncture, and giving fluids.

Hospice care was started in human medicine in the 1960s. It is a philosophy that promotes compassionate comfort care to patients at the end of their lives. The focus on hospice care is not to cure the animal but to lessen suffering and discomfort.

Hospice care allows patients to stay at home in familiar settings with family and pets instead of being hospitalized. Choosing to do this also requires much thoughtful discussion with your veterinarian and family; it may not be appropriate for all animals and for all family members. Some animals will pass away gently and peacefully, but this is not always the case. In those cases, humane euthanasia is advocated for avoiding unnecessary suffering.

Whichever way you choose, learning about the dying process may make the process less frightening if it is something you have never experienced before. The end of life is a stage that needs its own focused care.

How to Know if Hospice Care is Right For Your Pet

The first step is to make sure you have a very clear understanding of your pet's medical issues. You must discuss your pet's health with your veterinarian. It can be very helpful to make a list of your questions and concerns and then schedule the time to have them addressed. This way, you will have the knowledge you need to make any decisions that you must and to plan for your pet's care. By doing so, you will be acting in your pet's best interest as you have a full understanding of what is currently going on and what you may expect in the future.

Hospice care is best accomplished when the entire family and care-taking team understands and accepts the concept of hospice care. This is very important, as differences in personal philosophies can and will arise. People must take care with each other as well as with a beloved pet. A vital part of the caretaking team is your veterinarian and his or her staff. They are an invaluable part of making sure your pet receives the appropriate medical advice and care it needs.

Some of the major concerns in dealing with a pet in hospice care are quality-of-life issues, pain control, hygiene, hydration, nutrition, and the progression of the pet's disease or condition.

For more information about quality-of-life issues and a list of signs of pain, please see Chapter 20.

The caregiver or caregiving team should be well instructed in how to recognize signs that need to be reported to the veterinarian immediately. These signs include trouble breathing, continuous vomiting, seizures, fever, uncontrolled bleeding, restlessness, vocalizing, pain, difficulty urinating and/or defecating. Inability to sleep should as be addressed as soon as possible, as this is a sign of uncontrolled pain.

An addition, caregivers need to know how to administer medications, how to keep a pet comfortable and clean, how to provide adequate hydration and nutrition, how to provide bandage or wound care, and how to give other treatments that may be necessary.

Providing hospice care to your pet can be emotionally and physically demanding. Please see Chapter 4 for more information on how to take care of the caretaker.

The following is a beautiful paragraph that I found when grieving the death of my father, Samuel. May it bring you peace and comfort.

ALL IS WELL

Death is nothing at all. I have only slipped away into the next room. I am I and you are you. Whatever we were to each other that we are still. Call me by my old familiar name, speak to me in the easy way which you always used, put no difference into your tone; wear no forced air of solemnity or sorrow. Laugh as we always laughed at the little jokes we enjoyed together. Play, smile, think of me, pray for me. Let my name be ever the household word that it always was. Let it be spoken without an effort, without the ghost of a shadow on it. Life means all that it ever meant. It is the same as it ever was; there is absolutely unbroken continuity. Why should I be out of mind because I am out of sight? I am but waiting for you, for an interval, somewhere very near just around the corner. All, all is well.

Canon Scott Holland

CHAPTER 20
"When Will I Know It's Time?"
- End of Life Considerations

What you will learn in this chapter:

ᕮ **Where to begin in making an end-of-life decision**

ᕮ **What some signs of pain are**

ᕮ **What the process of euthanasia is**

ᕮ **What the grieving process is**

ᕮ **How pets left behind are affected**

ᕮ **How to cope with your grief**

ᕮ **How to memorialize your pet**

Even with thoughtful and consistent care, the day may come when you are faced with a difficult decision regarding your pet's life. There may be a number of reasons why you are considering the act of euthanasia. It is often difficult to make decisions when your heart is telling you one thing and your instincts possibly another. That is why it is best to make your decision based on what is best for your pet.

Learning about the dying process may make the process less frightening, if this is something you have never experienced before.

Where to Begin in Making an End-of-Life Decision

Solid information about what you are likely to encounter in the disease process may be helpful in making end-of-life decisions more manageable. Ask your veterinarian for specific information regarding your pet and its medical condition. Discuss with the veterinarian medical signs to watch for such as seizures, disorientation, difficulty breathing, painful abdomen, etc. It may be helpful to write down a list of signs that your pet may encounter so you can easily remember what to watch for.

One concept that may help in making decisions is asking, "What is my bottom line?" This is a guideline by which to measure your pet's quality of life or level of deterioration. For some, the bottom line is consistently refusing food; for others, it is difficulty breathing or hiding from or avoiding loved ones.

Examples of other situations to help gauge your pet's quality of life:

- Refusal to eat, no matter what is offered

- Incontinence, especially if the animal is immobile

- Inability to get up and walk

- Struggle to get comfortable or inability to get restful sleep

- Lack of interest in or interaction with family members or other pets, or both

Determining if your pet is feeling unwell can be difficult. Animals by nature try to hide this from people. In addition to signs of pain, you may notice the following:

- Lack of appetite. Some animals may turn their heads or move away from food put down near them. Food may make them feel nauseated.

- Vomiting or diarrhea, or both

- Lethargy

- Not acting like themselves. No interest in play or other pleasurable activities.

Signs of Pain

Signs of pain may include:

- Dilated pupils

- Pacing or restlessness

- Panting or heavy breathing

- Vocalizing: moaning, growling, crying

- Painful or pinched look to face

- Hunched back or tense belly

- Lameness, stumbling, or falling down

- Inability to stand

- Avoiding walking, jumping, using stairs, or moving around

- Not paying attention to detail, sound, or movement in the room

- Unusual aggressive behavior, such as growling or biting people or other pets. This could indicate pain or fear of pain when being touched.

- Difficulty sleeping

Although vocalizing can be a sign of pain, current thinking is that it may also be a way that dying animals communicate with us and other animals. By observing your pet's overall condition and attitude, you may be able to differentiate between the two.

Pain relief in veterinary patients is an art that requires up-to-date knowledge, clinical experience, and—most importantly—a doctor-client relationship based on honesty and trust. You should ask your veterinarian how to assess the signs of discomfort in your pet and to define the goals of treatment. It is appropriate to keep your veterinarian informed if you think that the pain medication is not adequately resolving your pet's discomfort and to request additional pain relief treatment options if needed. Please be your pet's advocate and speak up for pain medications! Your pet will be much more comfortable, and you will also feel a great sense of relief that your pet is no longer hurting.

Although there can be concern for side effects, there is a risk of side effects with all drugs. You can also lessen side effects by giving the drugs exactly as prescribed and reporting any concerns and adverse reactions to your veterinarian as soon as possible.

The Process of Euthanasia

The word euthanasia literally means "good death" in Greek. Veterinary medicine is fortunate in that it can offer this to our beloved pets to gently alleviate their suffering.

While no one can or should make the decision for you, there are questions to ask yourself that may be helpful in guiding you through this difficult decision-making process:

- How much time will additional treatments give my pet? What will the quality of life be during this time?

- Is there a reasonable chance for cure? For comfort? For control? Many disorders do not have a cure but can be properly controlled or managed.

ىك Do I have the emotional and financial resources to handle a long-term illness?

ىك Do I have the physical and emotional energy to attend to the extra care my pet will need?

ىك Is my relationship with my pet declining as I anticipate this loss?

ىك How many of my pet's usual activities are still possible?

ىك Is my pet suffering although physical pain may not be obvious?

It is often very helpful to talk to supportive friends and partners when making this decision. Stay away from people who tell you, "It's just a cat," or "It's just a dog." These people do not understand the love you and your pet share. There are many good books on the subject of pet loss. There are also knowledgeable and understanding people who run pet-loss support hotlines and websites. Talking to them may be helpful as you anticipate the loss of your friend. Please check the resource section of this book for more information.

Some people choose to bring their pets into the veterinary office or emergency hospital for this release from suffering, while others opt for an in-home euthanasia done by a veterinarian. Whichever way you choose, similar methods are used to ensure you and your pet have as peaceful an experience as possible.

Some people choose to be with their pet during euthanasia, while some cannot. Do not feel badly if you feel you cannot be present. Think of your pet's comfort—will your being upset be upsetting to your pet?

Another consideration is for families to discuss ahead of time who would like to be present. If small children are to be present, arrange ahead of time to have another adult available or a place the children can go if for any reason they change their minds during the procedure.

You will be asked to sign a form that gives the veterinarian permission to perform this procedure. Even if you have known your veterinarian for years, this is a standard legal practice because of the nature of the procedure being done and the fact that the injection used is a controlled substance. This means it is a highly regulated substance that is only available to veterinarians with a license to use it.

The billing of this procedure varies. You may ask to pay before the procedure, which ensures you can leave quickly afterward if you need to. Your vet may also agree to bill you. It is always a good idea to ask what the procedure is so that things will go as smoothly as possible.

To ensure easy access to a vein, many vets will place an IV catheter before the procedure. (Even if your veterinarian doesn't typically do this, you can request it.) Many older animals have problems with circulation. As a result, lack of good blood flow, in combination with disease or illness, can make it hard to find the vein. This can add stress to all involved. Often, the technician will ask to take your pet to a treatment area to place the IV catheter.

Also, as part of the procedure, many veterinarians will give a mild sedative to ensure the pet does not feel any stress. This also can give the owner a chance to spend time with his or her pet in a relaxed state.

Some animals have severe challenges with restraint at the end, especially animals that are having trouble breathing. Because of this, some veterinarians will offer to give the injection into the kidney. This causes an extremely quick passing or causes the animal to be very quickly sedated and relaxed. A second injection can then be given that will complete the euthanasia.

When you are ready, the veterinarian will inject the euthanasia solution into your pet's vein. Euthanasia solution is a pentobarbital, a barbiturate that is, in effect, an intravenous anesthetic drug. It is a concentrated form that first causes a deep anesthesia, then breathing to stop, after which the heart stops. It is not uncommon for an animal to have muscle spasms, and it may appear like it is gasping for breath. The diaphragm (a large muscle in the chest) may contract in response to lack of oxygen to the tissues, typically after the heart has stopped. This is an involuntary response from the body and is not in response to discomfort, pain, or the sensation of suffocating. In addition, the eyes may stay open.

Often, an animal will urinate or defecate or both after it has passed away. It is a good idea to have an absorbent towel or blanket under your pet during its passing. In the next hour or two, the animal's body will cool and the muscles will stiffen.

Some clinics are now making stamps of the front paw onto a keepsake card or making clay paw-print impressions as keepsakes.

Veterinary staff can discuss with you the different methods for aftercare. Some people choose to do a home burial, while for others, either private or group cremation is appropriate. As difficult as it may be, making these arrangements in advance may be easier than having to make them when you are actively grieving.

The Grieving Process

The process of grieving for a pet is perfectly normal. When people grieve for a loved one, there are several stages of grief that they may experience. These stages have been recognized as denial, sadness, depression, guilt, anger, and finally relief. (These stages are much less predictable in children, due to age and stages of maturity.) Grieving is a completely personal experience, which may be different with different people and with different pets. It may last for days or for years. Giving time to reflect and heal is a great gift you can offer to yourself or someone going through this process.

When Other Pets are Left Behind

Whether other family pets were the best of friends or merely tolerated each other, the loss of a pet does not go unnoticed by the remaining pets. For this reason, pay close attention to the physical and emotional states of animals left behind. Remaining pets need extra attention and reassurance at this time. The passing of a pet can cause the others to search for and even call out for a missing animal. Some animals may refuse to eat, become depressed or antisocial, vocalize more, or become restless when a companion pet is suddenly gone. They may spend more time in places they shared with the pet who is now gone.

It may be helpful for remaining animals to view and have the opportunity to spend time with a deceased pet, although we do not know if animals have the same concept of death that we do.

Occasionally and without solid explanation, some partnered animals will pass away shortly after their companion. They may be especially sensitive to death even with animals they may not have seemed to care for. In my personal experience, my cat Violet, who clearly disliked Alex, curled up in his bed with him before his in-home euthanasia and later remained by his body for about an hour after he passed away, standing as still as a sentry. Several years later, when Violet's longtime companion, Sesame, passed away, she went from being a healthy cat to succumbing to multiple health issues in six months.

It is very important to consider the feelings of remaining pets in the grieving process. It can be a time of uncertainty for them when a family pet is gone. Household dynamics, routines, and relationships may shift and rearrange with the passing of an animal. This is especially true with dogs because of their social ties with one another. The "pack" or group may now feel unstable, and as a result, there may be more competition for attention or resources, as well as more conflict or aggression.

Because animals pick up on our feelings easily, part of their depression may be in reaction to ours. To help the remaining pets through a difficult time, sticking to routines is vital. Keep feeding schedules, diet, exercise routines, and sleeping arrangements as much the same as possible. Keeping a routine will help the grieving pet owner as well as the remaining pets.

Coping With Your Grief and Memorializing Your Pet

Although grieving is an entirely personal experience, there are techniques that may be helpful to those experiencing it. Some things you may try are:

- Acknowledge your feelings, and allow yourself the time and space to come to terms with them. If you need to, take a little time away from work or commitments.

- Discuss your feelings with supportive friends, family members, or coworkers.

- Write about your feelings. Compose a story or poem about your pet. Record your feelings in a journal.

- Consider joining a pet-loss support group. Contact your veterinarian or local humane society to see if there is a group in your area. Some veterinary schools also offer this service.

- Read a book on the subject of pet loss. There are also excellent children's books on this subject.

- Search the Internet for pet-loss support groups.

- Memorialize your pet. Some ways to do this are:

    - Make a scrapbook, artwork, or specially framed picture of your pet.

    - Hold a celebration of life or memorial service with people who knew and loved your pet. Invite them to bring a can of food to donate to a shelter or rescue group in your pet's honor.

- ♥ Plant a tree, bush, or flower bed in your yard. If possible, choose a place your pet spent many happy hours. This offers you a place you can feel especially close to your pet.

- ♥ Make a donation in your pet's honor to help other, less fortunate animals.

- ♥ Donate a special piece of equipment or item from your local animal shelter's wish list in your pet's honor.

- ♥ Make a paw print out of clay.

- ♥ Clip some fur to keep in a special place.

- ♥ When the time is right, share your love again with a rescued animal that needs a good home.

Although this can be a tremendously sad time, rejoice in the fact that you gave of yourself to a beloved creature that needed your care. In time, you may find you are looking forward to beginning a new relationship with an animal. This time you need to grieve can vary, so give yourself as much time as you need. Whenever you choose, open your heart, and you will find another loving companion who will be very fortunate to share its life with you. The love you can give your pets is the greatest gift of all.

Resources

General Information:

- **Animal Wellness Magazine** – Website and magazine on a wide range of health issues for cats and dogs
  www.animalwellnessmagazine.com

- **Special Needs Pets** - Resources, information and support for special needs pets
  www.specialneedspets.org

- **Myrna Milani, DVM** - Written by veterinarian, consultant, teacher, and author, this site is dedicated to furthering our understanding of animal health, behavior, and the human-animal bond.
  www.MMilani.com

- **Jackson Galaxy** - Cat behaviorist and the host of Animal Planet's hit show *My Cat From Hell*. Website full of information on "catification", behavior, play therapy and many issues concerning cats.
  www.jacksongalaxy.com

- **Lost Pets** - Search and rescue information for lost pets. Information on the behavior of lost pets and how to find them.
  www.lostapet.org

- **Indoor Pet Initiative** - Information for improving the lives of indoor pets.
  www.indoorpet.osu.edu

- **ASPCA Animal Poison Control Center** - Resource for animal poison related emergencies, 24/7, 365 days a year. A $60 consultation fee may be applied to your credit card.
  (888) 426-4435 www.aspca.org/pet-care/animal-poison-control

- **Petfinder -** Find your next best friend online. Petfinder is the temporary home of 297,662 adoptable pets from 12,250 adoption groups.
  www.petfinder.com

Hospice/End of Life

- **Nikki Hospice Foundation for Pets** - Veterinary Hospice Care
  (707) 557-8595 www.pethospice.org

- **Spirits in Transition** - Options for end of life care for animal companions
  www.spiritsintransition.com

- **Angel Ashes -** Pet urns
  (800) 839-4604   www.angelashes.com

- **Rainbow Bridge Urns** - Pet memorialization items including urns, plaques, markers and keepsake jewelry.
  (877) 268-2912 www.rainbowbridgeurns.com

- **Petloss.com -** Compassionate website for pet lovers who are grieving. Offers support, advice, etc.
  www.petloss.com

- **Cornell University College of Veterinary Medicine -** Offers pet loss support hotline, support group and resources.
  (607) 253-3932   (Tuesday -Thursday 6 pm – 9 pm Eastern Time)
  www.vet.cornell.edu/org/petloss/

Organizations

- **American Holistic Veterinary Medical Association** - Information on holistic veterinary medicine, including how to find a holistic veterinarian in your area.
(410) 569-0795 www.ahvma.org

- **The Academy of Veterinary Homeopathy** - Information on homeopathy, including how to find names of veterinarians who practice homeopathy.
(305) 652-1590 www.theavh.org

- **International Veterinary Acupuncture Society** - Information on veterinary acupuncture, including information on how to find a practicing veterinarian
(303) 449-7936 www.ivas.org

- **Association for Pet Obesity Prevention** – Information and weight loss tools for cats and dogs
www.petobesityprevention.com

- **International Association for Animal Hospice and Palliative Care** – Information for veterinary professionals and pet parents
www.iaahpc.org

- **2nd Chance for Pets** - A non-profit organization devoted to protecting animal companions so they will receive lifetime care even if they are orphaned by their owners death or disability.
(408) 871-1133 www.2ndchance4pets.org

Nutrition

- **Feeding Your Cat: Know the Basics of Feline Nutrition** - Large amount of information on feline nutrition. Written by Lisa A. Pierson, DVM
www.catinfo.org

Reading a Pet Food Label
www.specialneedspets.org/nutrition.htm

Rad Cat - Premium Raw Food for Cats
Website includes information on transitioning your cat to raw food.
(503) 736-4649   www.radfood.com

Supplies

Dr. Goodpet - Natural pet pharmacy for dogs and cats. Sells nutritional supplements, homeopathic remedies, etc.
(800) 222-9932   www.goodpet.com

Trudell Medical International - maker of AeroKat and AeroDawg systems for use with MDIs (measured dose inhalers)
www.med.com/animal-health/aerokat

HomeoPet - Information and distribution of homeopathic remedies for animals
(800) 555-4461 www.homeopet.com

Standard Process - Nutritional supplements sold through health care professionals.
(800) 848-5061   www.standardprocess.com

Animal Apawthecary Herbs - (Sold through Animal Essentials)
(888) 551-0416   www.animalessentials.com

Bach® Flower Remedies - Makers of Rescue Remedy and 38 flower remedies
(800) 214- 2850   www.bachflower.com

Flower Essence Society – Articles, publications and information on flower essences
(800) 736-9222   www.flowersociety.org

- **PetEdge** - Supplier of pet supplies and products
  www.petedge.com

- **Supplies for Handicapped Pets** – Products, services and support for handicapped pets
  www.handicappedpets.com

- **Go-Cat Toys** - Interactive toys handcrafted in the USA. Maker of Da-Bird, Da Bee, and the Cat Catcher.
  (517) 543-7519   www.go-cat.com

- **Smart Cat Toys** - Makers of the Peek a Prize, Peek and Play toy box and other smart products for smart cats.
  (866) 31SMART (317-6278)   www.esmartcat.com

- **Kittywalk® Systems, Inc.** - Kittywalk designs and sells indoor and outdoor use pet products that are designed to keep your pet safe, but have fun doing it.
  (877) 548-8905 www.kittywalk.com

- **Habitat Haven** - Safe, healthy Habitats for Pets. Makers of products for cats, dogs and birds, including outdoor enclosures.
  (416) 466-8930 www.habitathaven.com

- **Purrfect Fence** - Cat Fencing system that safely keeps cats within a designated area. Excellent way for cats to get exercise and fresh air safely.
  (888) 280- 4066 www.PurrfectFence.com

- **Cat Fence-In** – Cat Containment System. Keeps cats safe in the backyard and keeps other cats out.
  (888) 738-9099   www.catfencein.com

- **The Smart Cat Box** – User and ecologically friendly cat box. Doubles as a urine collection system.
  (541) 563-4443 www.smartcatbox.com

idtag.com – Identification system includes online access to personal pet & owner profile, instant lost-pet alerts to shelters and 24-hour emergency customer support.
(866) 60-FOUND www.idtag.com

FasTags® - Shrinking ID tag to make at home for you dog or cat.
(866) 412-6860 www.fastags.com

HomeAgain - All inclusive pet recovery and protection service, using microchip technology.   Available through veterinarians.
(888) HOMEAGAIN (466-3242)   www.homeagain.com

Microchip ID - makers of Avid (American Veterinary Identification Device) microchips. Also available registration in PETtrac Recovery Network, global 24 hour database used by shelters and anyone finding a lost pet. Available through your veterinarian, shelters, etc.
(800) 336-2843 www.avidid.com

Drinkwell Pet Fountain (Veterinary Ventures) - Water fountains for cats and dogs that encourage drinking.
www.petsafe.net/drinkwell

SeniorPetProducts.com - Distributor of products for senior pets. Website includes articles, senior pet blog and information.
(800) 523-7979 www.seniorpetproducts.com

Precious Cat Litters - Dr. Elsey's Litterbox Solutions. Manufacturer of litter designed for cats that do not consistently use their litter box. Every bag has a free Dr. Elsey solutions booklet inside giving answers to solve litter box aversion.
(877) 311-2287 www.preciouscat.com

Ramp4Paws® **-** Roll out, roll up dog ramp.
(888) 654-7297 www.ramp4paws.com

- **Creative Pet Products** - Oral feeding syringes and pet first aid kits
  (877) 269-6911 www.petfirstaidkits.com

- **Cat Connection** - Products for cats including pill guns, etc.
  (830) 249-2532 www.catconnection.com

- **Greenies** – Makers of Pill Pockets® and other products for cats
  and dogs
  www.greenies.com

- **Cat Wheel Company** – Makers of the Cat Wheel – a safe way to
  get your cat to exercise more
  (949) 529-5531 catwheelcompany.com

- **American Red Cross** – Publishers of Cat and Dog First Aid Guides
  w/ DVD
  (202) 303-5000 www.redcross.org

Veterinary Care Financing

- **Care Credit** - CareCredit is a personal line of credit for health-
  care treatments, for people and pets. It can be very convenient in
  emergency situations.
  (866) 893-7864 www.carecredit.com

Dear Friend and Reader,

Thank you for reading *The Feel Better Book for Cats & Dogs*. I hope you enjoyed it and found it helpful when caring for your beloved furry friend. For more information on the care of diabetic pets please see my 1st book entitled *Sugarbabies – A Holistic Guide to Caring for Your Diabetic Pet.*

As an independent author I don't have the benefit of having a marketing department or the exposure of having my books on the shelves of large stores. If you enjoyed *The Feel Better Book for Cats & Dogs* and *Sugarbabies*, please help spread the word and support my writing by doing any of the following.

- Write a review for either or both books on Amazon.com. Reviews generate recommendations, will help my book show up in search results, will increase the number of people that click on a book and will ultimately generate sales.

- Recommend my books to your friends on social media sites such as Facebook, Pinterest and Twitter, among others

- Recommend my books to your local bookseller

- Donate a copy of my books to your local veterinary office, humane societies or rescue groups

- Donate a copy of my books to your local library or senior center

- Contact me with any marketing suggestions

Thank you very much,
Randi
catnurseoncall@hotmail.com
www.catnurseoncall.com

Made in the USA
San Bernardino, CA
29 April 2014